DIABETIC COOKBOOK FOR THE NEWLY DIAGNOSED

1500-Day Easy & Delicious Recipes for Diabetes, and Type 2 Diabetes Newly Diagnosed. Live Healthier without Sacrificing Taste. Includes 30-Day Meal Plan

Melissa Jordon

MELISSA JORDON
— *collection* —

Melissa Jordon
— collection —

DOWNLOAD YOUR GIFT NOW!

The bonus is **100% FREE.**
You don't need to enter any details except your name and email address.

To download your bonus scan the QR code below or go to

https://melissajordon.me/bonus-nd/

SCAN ME

ANTI-INFLAMMATORY Cookbook for Beginners

1200 Day Recipes to Improve Your Health, Reduce Inflammation and Lose Weight

Table of Contents

Introduction

What Is Diabetes?

Diabetes is a chronic metabolic illness marked by unsuitable hyperglycemia due to a lack of insulin or insulin resistance. Its adverse health effects can seriously reduce life expectancy significantly by ten years. Several lifestyle factors and dietary habits affect type 1 and type 2 diabetes incidence, such as types and amounts of food ingested, weight gain, obesity, physical activity, watching TV or sedentary time, and sleep quality.

Diabetes mellitus refers to a chronic disease that influences how the body utilizes energy food and is marked by abnormally high blood glucose levels. Insulin — the hormone the pancreas makes— allows glucose into body cells to provide energy.

When blood sugar levels rise after eating, your pancreas releases sufficient insulin into the blood. Insulin then reduces blood sugar to keep it in the normal range.

In people with diabetes, the pancreas cannot perform this fundamental function, or the body's cells do not respond adequately to the insulin produced.

The blood sugar level then increases, and sugar accumulates in the body and becomes toxic to the vital organs. Having a high glucose level in the blood can cause severe health problems. It can irreversibly cause severe damage to the eyes, kidneys, heart, and nerves.

Differences Between Diabetes Types

Diabetes Mellitus is the most common chronic endocrine disorder caused mainly by inflammation, according to recent high-quality research. There are three main types of diabetes:

a. *Type 1 Diabetes*

This type of diabetes is also known as juvenile-onset diabetes and insulin-dependent diabetes. It is a progressive autoimmune illness in which the body's immune system destroys the insulin-producing beta cells in the pancreas. Its onset is relatively swift. Genetic predisposition and environmental circumstances such as a childhood viral infection influence the onset of type 1 diabetes. It affects 5% of diabetic persons worldwide.

After the first six months of life, type 1 diabetes develops. Inherited gene mutations are frequently linked to early-onset type 1 diabetes (Diabetes, 2010).

People with type 1 diabetes depend on insulin shots to control their blood glucose levels since their bodies cannot produce insulin. To test for type 1 diabetes, it recommended that genetic testing for HNF1A (hepatocyte nuclear factor-1A) will be done to determine T1DM also evidence of non-insulin dependence, such as no ketosis in the absence of insulin treatment or satisfactory glycemic control on modest doses of insulin, indicates a positive result for T1DM.

b. *Type 2 Diabetes*

Type 2 diabetes is defined as having blood sugar levels greater than normal, which can lead to increased insulin resistance and insufficiency. Insulin is present, but it cannot do its job of facilitating the transport of glucose into cells. The onset of T2DM is among the older population above 30, accounting for 90% of all diabetes worldwide. Modifiable and non-modifiable risk factors mostly influence it.

Visceral adiposity (excess body fat) is highly linked to insulin resistance. It has diverse effects on muscle, fat, and liver cells. Insulin resistance in fat cells causes the mobilization of stored lipids and increased free fatty acids in circulation. Insulin resistance in muscle cells limits glucose uptake and prevents glucose from being stored as glycogen in the muscle.

These metabolic changes cause hyperglycemia. Insulin resistance, which causes high insulin and glucose levels in the blood, is thought to be the cause of metabolic syndrome and type 2 diabetes, as well as associated consequences. Insulin resistance causes decreased glycogen synthesis and a failure to control glucose production in liver cells, resulting in hypertension.

c. *Type 3 Diabetes*

Type 3 diabetes has been linked to an increased risk of Alzheimer's disease. Type 3 diabetes is mostly because of cognitive impairment and oxidative stress, which affects glucose metabolism. It's prevalent among people with Alzheimer's disease, such as insulin resistance and mitochondrial dysfunction. T3DM recent investigations indicate an underlying mechanistic linkage between metabolic alterations of carbs, lipids, proteins, and brain dysfunction.

Gestational diabetes is the high blood sugar that develops during pregnancy in women who did not have diabetes before becoming pregnant. Gestational diabetes is more frequent in the second or third trimester but can occur at any time of pregnancy and usually disappears after giving birth.

Women diagnosed with it are at higher risk of developing type 2 diabetes later in life, particularly for women with favoring factors (obesity, imbalanced diet, sedentary lifestyle, metabolic syndrome...).

How To Prevent And Control Diabetes

Let's start by saying that, unfortunately, as regards type 1 diabetes, it is not possible to implement preventive measures as, as we have seen, it is caused by environmental or genetic factors.

Even some factors triggering type 2 diabetes, such as advancing age, are not under the control of one's will.

However, many other factors can control or completely prevent the onset of type 2 diabetes.

The things to do to prevent its onset are:

• Try to lose weight if you are overweight or obese.

• Must try to keep blood pressure and cholesterol levels under control.

• Follow a healthy and balanced diet.

• Practice physical activity or sport at least three times a week.

• Stop smoking.

• Do an annual blood glucose check, if familiar.

Going into more detail and talking about nutrition, it should be emphasized that an incorrect diet is a very important risk factor for developing type 2 diabetes. A diet excessively high in saturated fat increases the possibility of contracting this disease.

When our body receives excess saturated fats, these interact with cellular receptors, leading to lipotoxicity and oxidative stress. Putting it as simply as possible, excess saturated fat causes irreparable damage to the cells of our body.

A risk factor, as we have seen, is a sedentary lifestyle. One of the most important causes of type 2 diabetes is an excessively sedentary lifestyle: there are now many studies showings how regular physical activity hinders the onset of this disease. Type 1 diabetics must regulate insulin therapy more closely to dietary intake and physical activity.

In contrast, for type 2 diabetics, who are also generally overweight or frankly obese, an adequate lifestyle assumes greater importance, which includes reduced calorie intake, especially from fat, and increased physical activity to improve blood sugar, dyslipidemia, and blood pressure levels.

Dietary Requirements For Diabetes

The food you introduce into your body plays a major role in treating diabetes. Carefully tracking your meals will help to improve your health and manage your blood glucose.

Of course, it is always best to consult a dietician specialising in diabetes so that you can tailor a meal plan suitable for your requirements.

Many diabetics, particularly those with Type 2 diabetes, are obese; therefore, weight loss and weight management are the most important issues.

Losing weight will greatly lower the risk of Type 2 diabetes and also prevents diabetes from getting worse. A healthy diet focused on weight loss can even boost the effects of medication. Lastly, achieving your optimal fitness level will enable you to lower your blood pressure, boost your energy levels and increase your life expectancy.

It is important to consider that genetics often plays a significant role in a person's ability to lose weight and may also govern the amount that can be lost.

Those with Type 2 diabetes generally lose less weight than those without diabetes. Knowing this information will keep you grounded and prevent you from becoming frustrated if you are not getting the results that you are hoping for.

a. *Monitor Your Calorie Intake*

A calorie is the unit of energy measurement, and the formula of weight loss is pretty simple: the number of calories you burn off through normal bodily functions and exercise should be more than the number of calories you take in from food. If you eat more calories than you burn off, you will naturally gain weight.

The amount of calories that your body needs depends on a variety of factors, including your age, your sex, your size and your body composition.

For instance, a pregnant or breastfeeding woman will need more calories than a man who works 8 hours a day behind a desk.

The three basic macronutrient food groups contain the most calories and proteins. It is necessary to cut 3,500 calories from your diet to lose one pound in weight, and it's healthy to aim for a weight loss of 1 – 2 lbs per week. That means cutting back by 500 – 1,000 calories daily from the basic calories your body needs to function.

b. Protein

The body requires a certain amount of protein to build and repair tissue. Children and young adults require more protein than adults because they are still growing. You can obtain protein from various sources, such as poultry, beef, pork, seafood, eggs, dairy products, legumes, soy, and nuts.

A diabetic needs to be careful in choosing his or her protein sources because animal proteins contain saturated fat.

The rule of thumb is to choose lean protein foods that can provide you with more protein and less fat and calorie content. An adult diabetic should eat no more than two medium-sized amounts of protein daily, including milk and legumes.

The recommended amount of protein in your daily calorie intake should be about 10 - 20% of total calories, although you should consider that protein can satisfy hunger better than carbohydrates and fat. This is useful when trying to lose weight as a diabetic since the feeling of satiety also helps stabilize blood sugar levels.

The following options are recommended for daily lean protein intake: baked or grilled lean beef, pork, veal or lamb, legumes including lentils, crab, lobster, prawns, low-fat milk, cheese and yogurt, skinless lean chicken or turkey meat, tofu, white fish, tuna, salmon, egg, and nuts. Avoid processed meats such as sausages, salami, Cheddar, feta, blue vein cream and Camembert cheeses.

c. Fat

It is very important to limit your fat intake, especially if you have diabetes. The maximum amount of fat in your daily calorie intake should be 30% of the total calories. Dietary fat has two main categories: saturated and unsaturated.

The "evil" fat is saturated fat and comes mainly from animal products. Butter, bacon, cream, cheese, and pastries contain saturated fat. Saturated fats that come from plant sources are coconut milk and palm oil. What makes saturated fat 'evil' is its effects on increasing your blood cholesterol level.

Ideally, the amount of saturated fat in your daily calorie intake should not be more than one-third of the 30% total.

Unsaturated fat comes from vegetable sources, including nuts and seeds and comes in monounsaturated and polyunsaturated. Monounsaturated fat will not increase your cholesterol level and is, therefore the "good" fat. You can get monounsaturated fat from canola oil, olive oil, almonds, peanuts and avocado. Polyunsaturated fat does not raise your cholesterol level, but it reduces your HDL or 'good' cholesterol. You can get polyunsaturated fat from soybeans, sunflowers, oily fish, and sesame oil.

You can reduce heart disease risk by adding essential fatty acids to your diet, particularly Omega-3. If you cannot maintain a regular intake of two to three servings of oily fish per week, or if you have problems with the absorption of Omega-3, you may benefit from fish oil supplements. Ensure that the capsules contain both EPA or eicosapentaenoic acid and DHA or docosahexaenoic acid. The recommended daily intake of fish oil is between 1,200 mg and 3,000 mg per day.

d. Carbohydrates

Ideally, diabetics should only eat complex carbohydrates, such as whole grains, brown rice, pasta and bread, since they are more nutritious, higher in fiber and lower in fat than refined carbohydrates. Your daily intake of complex carbohydrates should be around 40% of your daily calorie intake.

Fiber is not digestible, but it has several health benefits, including promoting a healthy digestive system and protecting against heart disease.

You can find fiber in whole foods such as grains, vegetables and fruits. Furthermore, fiber helps give you that feeling of being full and helps control the appetite.

That's a bonus when you're trying to lose weight.

Avoid simple carbohydrates that contain too many calories and not enough nutrients, such as soft drinks, alcoholic beverages, candies, jam, biscuits, cakes and refined white sugar, rice and pasta. Avoiding these foods lowers your glucose intake, thereby decreasing your blood glucose levels significantly. In addition, most simple or refined carbohydrates tend to be processed food, which is decidedly unhealthy, whether you are diabetic or not.

It is also advisable to check on the glycemic index or GI of the foods you eat because that will indicate how rapidly a particular carbohydrate food is digested. Complex carbohydrates take more time to be digested; therefore, the release of glucose into the bloodstream from these foods is much slower, which, in turn, buys time for the pancreas to keep up with its secretion of insulin.

However, that does not mean you can eat as many complex carbohydrates as you want because these still contain fat and may raise your blood glucose levels if eaten excessively. Make sure to control your portions by spreading carbohydrates evenly across breakfast, lunch and dinner.

e. Other Important Nutrients

Aside from monitoring your daily calorie intake of proteins, fats and carbohydrates, you should ensure that your diet includes sufficient vitamins and minerals, especially Vitamins A, B1 or thiamine, B2 or riboflavin, B6 or pyridoxine, pantothenic acid and biotin, B12, folic acid, Niacin, Vitamin C, D, E and K, calcium, phosphorus, magnesium, iodine, iron, sodium, chromium, chlorine, cobalt, tin, zinc and so on. These are all vital to maintaining the regular functions of the different cells in your body and helping to prevent infection.

You should also monitor your daily water intake because it is important to properly absorb nutrients. You should drink around 2 liters of water a day –about 6 to 8 glasses — and more if you have been exercising or in hot climates. As a diabetic, you should avoid sugary soft drinks and minimize your intake of caffeine and alcoholic beverages. Lemon water is a good way to detoxify and add some zest into plain old boring water, and herbal tea is considered well-accepted in the diabetic diet.

Helpful Tips For Switching To A Diabetic Diet

Your eating plan plays a key part in controlling your blood glucose level. Adhering to a good diet plan customized to your needs will help control your glucose levels and that's only the tip of the iceberg. The major part of an individual's health afflicted with diabetes is being overweight. The chances of getting diabetes increase more and more as an individual puts on weight. So controlling your eating habits can be the way to diminish the danger of diabetes.

For diabetes patients, having a healthy eating routine means eating to decrease the danger of complexities regularly related to their conditions, including coronary illness and stroke. Eating healthy includes a wide assortment of foods, including a range of vegetables, whole grains, natural products, non-fat dairy items, beans, lean meats, poultry, and fish.

You shouldn't eat big portions of every element stated above. However, a tad bit of various things is enough to optimize your health. Here are some step-by-step actions you can take.

a. Preparing A Meal Plan

When you commit to go on a healthy eating regimen suitable for a diabetic person, the first thing you have to do is to set up a meal plan. This will serve as your manual for how much and what sorts of food you can decide to eat at main meals and even at snack times.

First, ensure that your meal arrangement fits your calendar and dietary patterns. You won't ruin your eating regimen because your work routine clashes with your meal plan.

Remember your final objective: To keep your blood glucose at a sufficient level to keep up and stay healthy.

While setting up a dinner plan, make sure to adjust uptake and down take - food and exercise, respectively. Moreover, your physician may have recommended you take insulin or oral medicines to offer some assistance with managing your condition.

It is important to consider those medicines too when you arrange your meal plan, verifying that the food does not conflict with the types of medications you have to take.

b. Use The Diabetes Food Pyramid

The Diabetes Food Pyramid is made out of six food groups (organized by foods you should eat more of to foods you should eat less of due to their starch and protein content):

• Fats, sweets, and liquor

• Milk

• Meat, meat substitutes, and different proteins

• Fruits

• Vegetables

• Grains, beans, and Starchy vegetables

Fats, sweets, and liquor are the suggested foods that diabetes patients ought to maintain a safe distance from. The issue with diabetes includes a glitch in how bodies utilise glucose in the blood. It is because there is too much glucose in the blood due to an excessive amount of sugar-rich food. This causes a change in the hormone which directs glucose - insulin - is not able to adapt. On the other hand, the cells can be faulty so that despite the amount of insulin to handle the situation, the cells don't react.

With a specific end goal to control glucose levels in the blood circulatory system, controlling your eating routine is critical. The intake of fats, sweets, liquor and others, for the most part, "unhealthy" foods should be minimized and left just for unique occasions.

Concerning whatever is left of the food groups, here are the serving sizes suggested by physicians:

• Meat and Meat Substitutes: 4-6 oz. every day and spread between meals. This is comparable to 1/4 glass curds, 1 egg, 1 tbsp nutty spread, or 1/2 container tofu.

• Milk: 2-3 servings every day.

• Fruit: 2-4 servings every day.

• Vegetables: 3-5 servings every day.

• Grains and Starches: 6-11 servings daily, comparable to 1 slice of bread, 1/4 of a bagel.

Use this Diabetes Food Pyramid just as an aid in arranging your meals. If you need a more personalized choice, consult your dietician.

c. *Draw Lines On Your Plate*

Another great approach to guarantee that you are eating an adjusted eating routine is to draw a line over your plate. You can do this as you wait for a meal; you may even find this activity entertaining after sometime. The initial step is to imagine that you are drawing a line through the center point of your plate. At that point, divide one of the parts into two. At that point, fill this area with grains, for example, rice, pasta, potatoes, corn, or peas. The other area will contain your meat or meat substitute-meat, fish, poultry, or tofu. Next, fill half of your plate with vegetables. You can put their broccoli, carrots, cucumbers, a serving of mixed greens, tomatoes or cauliflower.

Last, include a glass of milk. You are ready to eat.

d. *Reading Food Labels*

With food labels, everything comes down to the "Nutrition Facts." It's that list of ingredient information found on the packets of foods sold in the market. Following this information will assist you with making wise decisions about the foods you purchase. The list will let you know what ingredients were used, the measure of calories, and other relevant data. Always take time to make a note of the nutrition label.

For example, an average food label would contain the sum of nutrition facts per serving of the particular product. Here is some information that you should look for on a label.

• Calories

• Total fat

• Saturated fat

• Cholesterol

• Sodium

• Total sugar

• Fiber

Use the nutrition facts found on food labels to look at similar sorts of foods and purchase the one that contains the least calories, lower fat, lower cholesterol, and so forth.

Consider "free" foods like sugar-free gelatin desserts, sugar-free ice cream, and sugarless gum.

Because they are called "free" does not mean they are completely free of calories, so read the name. Most free foods should have under 20 calories and 5 grams of sugar per serving. Another thing "no sugar included" means no sugar was included in the preparation and packing of the foods. The ingredients don't include sugar. Nonetheless, the food may be naturally high in starches, so consider this when purchasing food.

Fat-free foods could, in any case, contain heaps of sugars. So make certain to pay consideration to the label. Purchasing fat-free foods rather than customary foods docs not imply that you are settling on a wise decision.

e. *Having Diabetes Does Not Imply That You Can't Ever Have Desserts.*

Imagine how awful life can be for someone with a sweetish who also has diabetes. Be that as it may, as long as you keep your intake of desserts with some restraint, there is no reason you need to cut off sugar from your life entirely. Glucose (sugar) is still the essential wellspring of energy the body needs.

How To Deal With Diabetes When We Are First Diagnosed With It

If you have been newly diagnosed with diabetes, you may wonder what treatments are available. Let's review the most common ways of treating this disease.

a. *Diet*

Seeking nutrition education from a nutrition expert is highly effective. Registered dietitians, certified diabetes educators, are the best source of science-based, credible diabetes nutrition education. They can provide medical nutrition therapy (MNT), a diet specifically created and customized for those with diabetes. Research has found that MNT from a registered dietitian can help lower hemoglobin A1c for people with type 2 diabetes by 0.3 to 2.0 percent, according to the American Diabetes Association.

It's important to realize there isn't only one way to succeed when modifying what you eat to manage diabetes. Several different meal-planning strategies and methods have been found to work. Of those that have been most studied, the Mediterranean diet, the DASH diet, and vegetarian and plant-based foods have all been shown to be helpful in both preventing diabetes and managing it.

b. *Physical Activity*

Physical activity encompasses many different types of movement and is critical to include in all diabetes management plans. Participating in a structured exercise plan for at least eight consecutive weeks has been found to reduce hemoglobin A1c levels by up to 0.66 percent, even if there is no change in weight, according to research published in 2001 in the Journal of the American Medical

Association. This is significant and should be a big motivation to get you moving. As you lose weight, your A1c should go down even more.

The goal is for adults with type 2 diabetes to engage in 150 minutes weekly physical activity at least three days a week. To experience the most benefits, it's recommended to go no more than two consecutive days without exercising.

While this physical activity recommendation can seem daunting if you are not currently doing much exercise, be encouraged that it's completely fine to start where you are and continue to increase the intensity and duration as you are able. Flexibility, strength, and balance training are also helpful.

c. *Medication*

Depending on your situation, your healthcare provider may recommend medication. Please don't view a medication prescription as a failure. Over the years, as I have taught diabetes education, I've had patients compare their situations—some were on no medications, some were on insulin, some were on multiple oral medications—and judge themselves based on this comparison.

It is a myth that people who are not taking any medications have better blood sugar numbers than those who take medications. One goal is to keep your blood sugar levels as well controlled as possible because that is the number one way to prevent complications related to diabetes. Taking diabetes medications does not mean you will always have to be on them, nor does it mean you have failed in your efforts to control your blood sugar. It means, at that moment, your healthcare team believes you need them. It is important to ask questions about how to take your medication properly and to be sure to do so.

While there is no cure for diabetes, you absolutely can manage and control it by paying attention to what you eat, increasing your physical activity, maintaining a healthy weight, and taking medication, if necessary. Know your options and make the best plan for yourself with your healthcare team.

Shopping List – What To Eat And What To Avoid

a. *Foods To Eat*

Some of the best foods to consume when you have diabetes include:

- Lean protein foods (tempeh, tofu, lean red meat, seafood, skinless poultry, etc.)
- fruits (peaches, pears, melons, berries, oranges, apples, etc.)
- vegetables (zucchini, cucumbers, spinach, cauliflower, broccoli, etc.)
- whole grains (farro, brown rice, oats, couscous, quinoa, etc.)
- legumes (chickpeas, lentils, beans, etc.)

- nuts (cashews, macadamia nuts, pistachios, walnuts, almonds, etc.)
- seeds (hemp seeds, flax seeds, pumpkin seeds, chia seeds, etc.)
- Healthy fats (sesame oil, canola oil, avocados, olive oil, etc.)
- Beverages (vegetable juice, unsweetened tea, black coffee, water, etc.)

b. Foods To Avoid

Some of the foods and beverages that you should stay away from when you have diabetes include:

- High-fat meat (dark chicken meat, poultry skin, fatty cuts of pork, etc.)
- Full-fat dairy (sour cream, cheese, whole milk, etc.)
- Sweets (desserts, ice cream, baked goods, candy, etc.)
- Sugar-rich beverages (sports drinks, sweet tea, soda, juice, etc.)
- Sweeteners (molasses, brown sugar, table sugar, etc.)
- Trans fats (fried foods, vegetable shortening, coffee creamers, etc.)
- Processed foods (processed meat, microwave popcorn, etc.)

CHAPTER 1: Breakfast

1. Spicy Avocado Deviled Eggs

Preparation time: 10 minutes

Cooking time: 0 minutes

Servings: 12

Ingredients:

- 6 hard-boiled eggs, peeled and halved lengthwise
- 1 ripe avocado, halved and pitted
- 1 tbsp Dijon mustard
- 1 tbsp sour cream
- 1½ tsps. freshly squeezed lemon juice
- ½ tsp garlic powder
- ½ tsp salt
- ¼ tsp red pepper flakes

Directions:

1. Scoop egg yolks into a small bowl.

2. Scoop avocado flesh in a bowl with yolks.

3. Add mustard, sour cream, lemon juice, garlic powder, salt, and red pepper flakes.

4. Whisk, and mash the mixture until thoroughly combined and creamy.

5. Arrange eggs on a plate. Spoon equal amounts of the yolk-avocado mixture into each egg. Refrigerate bee serving, if desired.

Per serving: Calories: 124 kcal; Fat: 9 g; Carbs: 3 g; Protein: 7 g; Sugar: 1 g

2. Chia Chocolate Pudding

Preparation time: 5 minutes + 2-8 hours to chill

Cooking time: 0 minutes

Servings: 2-3

Ingredients:

- ½ cup unsweetened almond milk
- ½ cup nonfat plain Greek yogurt
- 2 tbsps. chia seeds
- 1 tbsp vanilla whey Sugar 1g, Protein
- 1 tsp unsweetened cocoa powder
- ½ tsp stevia or no-calorie sweetener

Directions:

1. Combine almond milk, yogurt, chia seeds, whey, cocoa powder, and stevia in a canning jar.

2. Seal with a lid and let sit in the refrigerator overnight.

3. Enjoy straight from the jar or in a separate bowl if you consume a smaller serving.

Per serving: Calories: 257 kcal; Fat: 12 g; Carbs: 21 g; Protein: 25 g; Sugar: 5 g

3. Perfect Hard-boiled Eggs

Preparation time: 15 minutes or fewer

Cooking time: 2½ hours on high

Servings: 2

Ingredients:

- 6 large eggs
- 1 tablespoon distilled white vinegar

Directions:

1. Place eggs along the bottom of the slow cooker, making sure none are stacked.

2. Add enough water to the slow cooker to just cover the eggs. Add vinegar.

3. Cover the cooker and set it to high. Cook for 2½ hours. Let cool before serving.

Per serving: Calories: 74 kcal; Fat: 5 g; Carbs: 1 g; Protein: 6 g; Sugar: 1 g

4. Raspberry Almond Oatmeal

Preparation time: 5 minutes

Cooking time: 10 minutes

Servings: 2

Ingredients:

- ½ cup rolled oats
- 1 cup almond milk
- ½ cup water
- 2 tablespoons flax seeds, ground
- 1 ripe banana, mashed
- 2 tablespoons maple syrup
- ½ cup fresh raspberries
- 2 tablespoons sliced almonds

Directions:

1. In a saucepan, Combine almond milk with water and Boil.

2. Stir in rolled oats, banana and flax seeds and cook for 5-8 minutes on low heat until thick and creamy.

3. Remove from heat, and stir in maple syrup.

4. Spoon mixture into two serving bowls and top with fresh raspberries and sliced almonds.

Per serving: Calories: 273 kcal; Fat: 18 g; Carbs: 27 g; Protein: 5 g; Sugar: 1 g

5. Apple Oats

Preparation time: 5 minutes

Cooking time: 5 minutes

Servings: 2

Ingredients:

- ½ cup oats
- 1 cup water
- 1 apple, chopped
- 1 tsp olive oil
- ½ tsp vanilla extract

Directions:

1. Pour olive oil into a saucepan and add oats. Cook them for 2 minutes, and stir constantly.

2. Add water and mix up.

3. Cook oats for 5 minutes.

4. Add apples and vanilla. Stir mixture.

Per serving: Calories: 169 kcal; Fat: 4 g; Carbs: 30 g; Protein: 3 g; Sugar: 1 g

6. Rajun' Cajun Roll-Ups

Preparation time: 5 minutes

Cooking time: 0 minutes

Servings: 2-3

Ingredients:

- 4 slices nitrate-free Cajun deli turkey
- 4 tsps. spicy mustard, divided
- 4 slices pepper Jack cheese
- ½ steak tomato, seeded and diced
- ¼ red onion, thinly sliced

- 2 cups shredded lettuce
- ½ avocado, diced
- ¼ cup chopped banana peppers

Directions:

1. Lay out a slice of deli turkey and spread it with 1 tsp of mustard.

2. Top with a slice of cheese, tomato, onion slices, shredded lettuce, diced avocado and banana peppers.

3. Wrap deli turkey tightly, but delicately, around the filling, and pin it with a toothpick.

4. Repeat the process three times with the remaining ingredients, and serve.

Per serving: Calories: 152 kcal; Fat: 9 g; Carbs: 6 g; Protein: 10 g; Sugar: 1 g

7. Breakfast Hash

Preparation time: 15 minutes

Cooking time: 25 minutes

Servings: 2

Ingredients:

- Nonstick cooking spray
- 2 large sweet potatoes,
- 1 scallion, finely chopped
- ¼ tsp salt
- ½ tsp freshly ground black pepper
- 8 oz extra-lean ground beef (96% or leaner)
- 1 medium onion, diced
- 2 garlic cloves, minced
- 1 red bell pepper, diced
- ¼ tsp ground cumin
- ¼ tsp paprika
- 2 cups coarsely chopped kale leaves
- ¾ cup shredded reduced-fat Cheddar cheese
- 4 large eggs

Directions:

1. Coat skillet with cooking spray, then heat over medium heat. Add sweet potatoes, scallion, salt, and pepper. Sauté for 10 minutes, stirring

2. Add beef, onion, garlic, bell pepper, cumin, and paprika. Sauté, frequently stirring, for about 4

minutes or until meat browns. Add kale to skillet and stir until wilted. Sprinkle with Cheddar cheese.

3. Make four wells in the hash mixture and crack an egg into each. Cover the eggs and cook until the white is fully cooked and the yolk is to your liking. Divide into four storage containers.

Per serving: Calories: 323 kcal; Fat: 2 g; Carbs: 23 g; Protein: 25 g; Sugar: 1 g

8. German Chocolate Cake Protein Oats

Preparation time: 15 minutes or fewer

Cooking time: 6-8 hours on low

Servings: 2

Ingredients:

- 1 tablespoon coconut oil
- 2 cups rolled oats
- 2½ cups water
- 2 cups full-fat coconut milk
- ¼ cup unsweetened cacao powder
- 2 tablespoons collagen peptides
- ¼ teaspoon salt
- 2 tablespoons pecans
- 2 tablespoons unsweetened shredded coconut

Directions:

1. Coat the slow cooker with coconut oil.

2. Combine oats, water, coconut milk, cacao powder, collagen peptides, and salt in your slow cooker. Stir to combine.

3. Cover the cooker and set it to low. Cook for 6 - 8 hours.

4. Sprinkle pecans and coconut on top and serve.

Per serving: Calories: 457 kcal; Fat: 33 g; Carbs: 36 g; Protein: 10 g; Sugar: 3 g

9. Cranberry Muesli

Preparation time: 5 minutes

Cooking time: 10 minutes

Servings: 2

Ingredients:

- 6 tablespoons rolled oats (not steel cut or quick cooking)
- 2 tablespoons dried cranberries
- ½ cup low-fat plain yoghurt
- ½ cup cranberry juice (either unsweetened or sweetened with fruit juice)
- 1 tablespoon sunflower seeds (unsalted)
- 1 tablespoon wheat germ
- 2 teaspoons honey
- ¼ teaspoon vanilla extract
- Dash of salt

Directions:

1. Mix all the ingredients.

2. Cover and refrigerate overnight (between 8 hours and one day). Serve as is or with soy/cow/almond milk.

Per serving: Calories: 160 kcal; Fat: 3 g; Carbs: 26 g; Protein: 7 g; Sugar: 1 g

10. Southwest Deviled Eggs

Preparation time: 10 minutes

Cooking time: 0 minutes

Servings: 2-3

Ingredients:

- 6 large hard-boiled eggs
- 2 tbsps. low-fat, plain Greek yogurt
- ¼ tsp spicy mustard
- 1/8 tsp salt
- ½ tsp Taco Seasoning

Directions:

1. Peel eggs, and halve them lengthwise.

2. Remove yolks, and transfer to a small bowl, setting whites aside.

3. Add yogurt, spicy mustard, salt, and taco seasoning to bowl with yolks, and mash everything together.

4. Spoon mixture in egg white halves, and serve.

Per serving: Calories: 83 kcal; Fat: 5 g; Carbs: 1 g; Protein: 7 g; Sugar: 1 g

11. Savory Yogurt Bowls

Preparation time: 15 minutes

Cooking time: 0 minutes

Servings: 2

Ingredients:

- 1 medium cucumber, diced
- ½ cup pitted Kalamata olives, halved 2 tbsp fresh lemon juice
- 1 tbsp Extra-virgin olive oil
- 1 tsp dried oregano
- ¼ tsp freshly ground black pepper 2 cups nonfat plain Greek yogurt
- ½ cup slivered almonds

Directions:

1. Mix cucumber, olives, lemon juice, oil, and pepper in a small bowl.

2. Divide yogurt evenly among four storage containers. Top with cucumber-olive mix and almonds.

Per serving: Calories: 240 kcal; Fat: 16 g; Carbs: 10 g; Protein: 16 g; Sugar: 1 g

12. Sweet Potato Home Fries

Preparation time: 15 minutes or fewer

Cooking time: 6-8 hours on low

Servings: 2

Ingredients:

- 3 tablespoons extra-virgin olive oil, + more for coating slow cooker
- 2 pounds sweet potatoes, diced
- 1 red bell pepper, seeded and diced
- ½ medium onion, finely diced
- 1 teaspoon garlic powder
- 1 teaspoon salt
- 1 teaspoon dried rosemary, minced
- ½ teaspoon pepper

Directions:

1. Coat the slow cooker with a thin layer of olive oil.

2. Put sweet potatoes in the slow cooker, along with red bell pepper and onion. Drizzle olive oil as evenly as possible over vegetables.

3. Sprinkle in garlic powder, salt, rosemary, and pepper. Toss evenly to coat sweet potatoes in oil and seasonings.

4. Cover the cooker and set it to low. Cook for 6 - 8 hours and serve.

Per serving: Calories: 296 kcal; Fat: 11 g; Carbs: 48 g; Protein: 4 g; Sugar: 10 g

13. Cauliflower Mac & Cheese

Preparation time: 15 minutes

Cooking time: 20 minutes

Servings: 4

Ingredients:

- Cauliflower (1 head)
- Butter (3 tbsp.)
- Unsweetened almond milk (.25 cup)
- Heavy cream (.25 cup)
- Cheddar cheese (1 cup)

Directions:

1. Use a sharp knife to slice cauliflower into small florets. Shred cheese. Prepare oven to reach 450º Fahrenheit. Cover a baking pan with a layer of parchment baking paper or foil.

2. Add two tbsps. of butter to pan and melt. Add florets, butter, salt, and pepper together. Place cauliflower on a baking pan and roast for 10 to 15 minutes.

3. Warm up the rest of the butter, milk, heavy cream, and cheese in the microwave or double boiler. Pour cheese over cauliflower and serve.

Per serving: Calories: 294 kcal; Fat: 23 g; Carbs: 7 g; Protein: 11 g; Sugar: 1 g

14. Granola Parfait

Preparation time: 10 minutes

Cooking time: 0 minutes

Servings: 2

Ingredients:

- ½ cup low-fat yogurt
- 4 tbsp granola

Directions:

1. Put ½ tbsp of granola in every glass.

2. Then add two tbsp of low-fat yogurt.

3. Repeat the steps till you use all ingredients.

4. Store parfait in the fridge for up to 2 hours.

Per serving: Calories: 79 kcal; Fat: 8 g; Carbs: 21 g; Protein: 8 g; Sugar: 1 g

15. Flaxseed Banana Muffins

Preparation time: 5 minutes

Cooking time: 30 minutes

Servings: 2

Ingredients:

- ¼ cup flax seeds, ground
- 1 cup all-purpose flour
- 1 cup whole wheat flour
- 1 teaspoon baking soda
- 1 pinch salt
- 1 teaspoon cinnamon powder
- 1 cup shredded coconut
- 3 ripe bananas, mashed
- ¼ cup coconut oil
- 1 cup water
- ¼ cup maple syrup

Directions:

1. Combine flax seeds with flour, baking soda, salt, cinnamon and shredded coconut.

2. Mix bananas with coconut oil, water, and maple syrup in a different bowl. Pour this mixture over dry ingredients and mix very well.

3. Spoon batter into your muffin cups lined with muffin papers and bake them in preheated oven at 350F for 25 minutes or 'til golden brown and fragrant.

4. Let them cool in the pan before serving.

Per serving: Calories: 130 kcal; Fat: 5 g; Carbs: 19 g; Protein: 2 g; Sugar: 1 g

16. Cinnamon Fried Bananas

Preparation time: 7 minutes

Cooking time: 5 minutes

Servings: 2-3

Ingredients:

- 1 cup panko breadcrumbs
- tbsp. cinnamon
- ½ cups almond flour
- egg whites
- ripe bananas
- tbsp. coconut oil

Directions:

1. Heat coconut oil and add breadcrumbs, mix for around 3 minutes until golden, then pour it into a bowl.

2. Peel and cut bananas in half.

3. Roll half of each banana in flour, eggs, and crumb mixture.

4. Place in Smart Air Fryer Oven. Cook for 10 minutes at 280 °F.

Per serving: Calories: 221 kcal; Fat: 9 g; Carbs: 5 g; Protein: 4 g; Sugar: 1 g

17. Super-Simple Granola

Preparation time: 10 minutes

Cooking time: 25 minutes

Servings: 2

Ingredients:

- ¼ cup extra-virgin olive oil
- ¼ cup honey
- ½ tsp ground cinnamon
- ½ tsp vanilla extract
- ¼ tsp salt
- 2 cups rolled oats
- ½ cup chopped walnuts
- ½ cup slivered almonds

Directions:

1. Preheat oven to 350°F. Line the pan with parchment paper or a silicone baking mat.

(Alternatively, you can coat the pan with cooking to prevent sticking.)

2. Whisk oil, honey, cinnamon, vanilla, and salt in a large bowl. Add oats, walnuts, and almonds. Stir to coat. Spread mixture out of prepared sheet pan.

3. Bake for 20 minutes. Let cool.

Per serving: Calories: 254 kcal; Fat: 16 g; Carbs: 25 g; Protein: 5 g; Sugar: 1 g

18.   Simple Steel-Cut Oats

Preparation time: 15 minutes or fewer

Cooking time: 6 - 8 hours on warm

Servings: 2

Ingredients:

- 1 tablespoon coconut oil
- 4 cups boiling water
- ½ teaspoon salt
- 1 cup steel-cut oats

Directions:

1. Coat the slow cooker with coconut oil.

2. In your slow cooker, combine boiling water, salt, and oats.

3. Cover the cooker and set it to warm (or low if there is no warm setting). Cook for 6 - 8 hours and serve.

Per serving: Calories: 172 kcal; Fat: 6 g; Carbs: 27 g; Protein: 6 g; Sugar: 0 g

19.   Melting Tuna and Cheese Toasties

Preparation time: 10 minutes

Cooking time: 8 minutes

Servings: 2-3

Ingredients:

- 6oz. canned line caught tuna in water
- tsp. lemon juice
- 1/2 tbsp. olive oil
- A pinch of sea salt and pepper
- 1/4 cooked yellow corn
- 4 slices of whole-meal bread
- ½ cup low-fat cheddar

Directions:

1. Preheat the broiler/grill to its highest setting.

2. Drain tuna and flake in a bowl.

3. Mix in lemon juice and olive oil.

4. Season with salt and pepper

5. Add in corn.

6. Toast bread under the grill until it's nicely browned on both sides, and spread tuna mixture on top, right up to the edges of the toast.

7. Grate over cheese and grill until cheese is bubbling.

8. Slice in half, grab a plate and enjoy.

Per serving: Calories: 170 kcal; Fat: 4 g; Carbs: 14 g; Protein: 15 g; Sugar: 2 g

20.   Whole Grain Pancakes

Preparation time: 5 minutes

Cooking time: 10 minutes

Servings: 2

Ingredients:

- ½ tsp baking powder
- ¼ cup skim milk
- 1 cup whole-grain wheat flour
- 2 tsp liquid honey
- 1 tsp olive oil

Directions:

1. Mix baking powder and flour in a bowl.

2. Add skim milk and olive oil. Whisk the mixture well.

3. Preheat a nonstick skillet and pour a small amount of dough inside in the shape of a pancake. Cook for 2 minutes from each side until the pancake is golden brown.

4. Top-cooked pancakes with liquid honey.

Per serving: Calories: 129 kcal; Fat: 2 g; Carbs: 26 g; Protein: 5 g; Sugar: 1 g

CHAPTER 2: Grains, Beans And Legumes

21. Cauliflower Fried Rice

Preparation time: 15 minutes

Cooking time: 8 minutes

Servings: 2-3

Ingredients:

- 1 tsp sesame oil, plus 1 tbsp
- 2 large eggs, beaten
- 4 cups cauliflower rice
- 1 cup frozen mixed vegetables
- 2 garlic cloves, minced
- 2 tbsps. low-sodium soy sauce
- 2 scallions, diced

Directions:

1. Heat sesame oil. Add eggs, and stir until cooked. Set aside.

2. Heat the remaining tbsp of oil in the same skillet over medium heat. Add cauliflower rice, mixed vegetables, garlic, soy sauce, scallions, and eggs. Cook, stirring, until well combined and cauliflower is soft, 4 minutes, and serve. Please make sure not to overcook cauliflower, or it will become soggy.

Per serving: Calories: 121 kcal; Fat: 7 g; Carbs: 9 g; Protein: 6 g; Sugar: 3 g

22. Cauliflower Rice

Preparation time: 5 minutes

Cooking time: 5 minutes

Servings: 2-3

Ingredients:

- 1 cauliflower head
- 1 tsp extra-virgin olive oil

Directions:

1. Prepare cauliflower head by removing stems and leaves. Cut it into four large pieces.

2. Put cauliflower in the food processor, then pulse until it breaks down into pieces of rice. You may need to remove any leftover pieces of stem.

Alternatively, you can use a box grater to shred cauliflower.

3. Transfer riced cauliflower to a plate or bowl and pat it dry with a paper towel.

4. Heat olive oil. When the oil is hot, add cauliflower. Sauté 5 - 6 minutes, or until tender. Alternatively, steam cauliflower rice and drain off any excess liquid bee serving.

Per serving: Calories: 32 kcal; Fat: 0 g; Carbs: 2 g; Protein: 1 g; Sugar: 1 g

23. Black Bean Quesadillas

Preparation time: 10 minutes

Cooking time: 12 minutes

Servings: 4

Ingredients:

- black beans (1 (28 oz)
- tomatoes (1/2 cup)
- cilantro (3 tbs)
- black olives
- cumin (1/Two teaspoon)
- fat-free Monterey Jack cheese (1/2 cup)
- fresh spinach leaves (Two cups)
- whole wheat tortillas (8 rounds)

Directions:

1. Preheat oven to 350 degrees. In a bowl, mash beans until smooth but slightly chunky.

2. Stir in tomato, cilantro and olives, and cumin. Spread the mixture evenly onto four tortillas. Sprinkle with cheese and spinach.

3. Put the remaining tortillas on top. Bake tortillas on a baking sheet that is not greased for 12 minutes.

4. Cut into wedges and serve.

Per serving: Calories: 203 kcal; Fat: 1 g; Carbs: 37 g; Protein: 12 g; Sugar: 2 g

24. Slow Cooker Boston Beans

Preparation time: 5 minutes

Cooking time: 15 minutes

Servings: 2-3

Ingredients:

- 1 pound – White Northern beans, dry.
- 1 cup – Onion, finely chopped
- 2 slices – of turkey bacon, chopped
- 1 cup – Dark molasses
- 2 tbsps. – Ketchup
- 1 tbsp – Mustard
- ½ tsp – Salt
- ½ tsp – Pepper
- 3 cups – Water

Directions:

1. In a medium bowl, soak beans. Drain beans and keep aside.

2. Put all ingredients in the slow cooker. Set the timer for 30 minutes and start cooking. Serve hot.

Per serving: Calories: 134 kcal; Fat: 6 g; Carbs: 12 g; Protein: 1 g; Sugar: 8 g

25. Pinto Beans

Preparation time: 6 minutes

Cooking time: 55 minutes

Servings: 10

Ingredients:

- 2 c. pinto beans, dried
- 1 medium white onion
- 1 1/2 teaspoons minced garlic
- 3/4 teaspoon salt
- 1/4 tsp. ground black pepper
- 1 tsp. red chili powder
- 1/4 tsp. cumin
- 1 tbsp. olive oil
- 1 tsp. chopped cilantro
- 5 1/2 c. vegetable stock

Directions:

1. Plugin the instant pot, insert the inner pot, press the sauté/simmer button, add oil and when hot, add onion and garlic, then cook for 3 minutes or until onions begin to soften.

2. Add the remaining ingredients, stir well, press the cancel button, shut the instant pot with its lid, and seal it.

3. Click the manual button, press the timer to set the cooking time to 45 minutes and cook at high pressure.

4. Once done, click the cancel button and do a natural pressure release for 10 minutes until the pressure nob drops.

5. Open the instant pot, spoon beans into the plates, and serve.

Per serving: Calories: 107 kcal; Fat: 33 g; Carbs: 12 g; Protein: 12 g; Sugar: 3 g

26. Sweet Potato And Black Bean Chili

Preparation time: 10 minutes

Cooking time: 20 minutes

Servings: 8

Ingredients:

- 2 tbsps. avocado oil
- 1 red onion, diced
- 5 garlic cloves, minced
- 1 red bell pepper, diced
- 1 green bell pepper, diced
- 3 cups cooked sweet potato cubes
- 3 cups cooked black beans,
- 2 cups vegetable broth
- 1 (28-ounce) can of diced tomatoes with juice
- 1 tbsp freshly squeezed lime juice
- 1 tbsp chili powder
- 1 tsp cocoa powder
- 1 tsp ground cumin
- 1 tsp salt
- ½ tsp ground cinnamon
- ¼ tsp cayenne pepper
- ¼ tsp dried oregano

Directions:

1. Heat pot and warm avocado oil.

2. Add onion and garlic, then sauté 2 minutes.

3. Stir red and green bell pepper, and sauté 3 minutes until soft.

4. Add sweet potato, beans, broth, tomatoes, lime juice, chili powder, cocoa powder, cumin, salt, cinnamon, cayenne pepper, and oregano, and stir to combine. Bring to a simmer, and cook for 15 minutes. Serve immediately.

Per serving: Calories: 160 kcal; Fat: 4 g; Carbs: 29 g; Protein: 4 g; Sugar: 1 g

27. Wild Rice Harvest Soup

Preparation time: 15 minutes

Cooking time: 30 minutes

Servings: 6

Ingredients:

- 1 cup wild rice
- 4 cups vegetable broth
- 5 carrots, chopped in disks
- 5 celery stalks, chopped
- 8 ounces cremini mushrooms, sliced
- 1 small yellow onion, diced
- 4 garlic cloves, minced
- 1 tsp sea salt
- 1 tsp dried thyme
- ½ tsp dried rosemary
- 1½ cups coconut milk

Directions:

1. In Instant Pot, combine wild rice, broth, carrots, celery, mushrooms, onion, garlic, salt, thyme, and rosemary. Lock lid.

2. Select Pressure Cook, and cook at high for 30 minutes.

3. When cooking is complete, use a quick release.

4. Remove the lid and Stir the coconut milk. Serve warm.

Per serving: Calories: 259 kcal; Fat: 12 g; Carbs: 33 g; Protein: 7 g; Sugar: 1 g

28. Sweetened Brown Rice

Preparation time: 10 minutes

Cooking time: 45-60 minutes

Servings: 8

Ingredients:

- 1½ cups soy milk
- 1½ cups water
- 1 cup brown rice
- 1 tbsp honey
- ¼ tsp nutmeg
- Fresh fruit (optional)

Directions:

1. Put all ingredients, excluding fresh fruit, in a medium-sized saucepan; place mixture to a slow simmer, then cover using a tight-fitting lid.

2. Simmer for 45-60 minutes up until rice is tender and done. Serve in bowls, topped with your favorite fresh fruit.

Per serving: Calories: 155 kcal; Fat: 2 g; Carbs: 13 g; Protein: 3 g; Sugar: 3 g

29. Lemon Chicken and Rice

Preparation time: 5 minutes

Cooking time: 20 minutes

Servings: 2

Ingredients:

- 2 tbsp butter
- 1 lb chicken breasts, cut into strips, boneless and skinless
- 1 chopped onion
- 1 thinly sliced carrot
- 2 minced garlic cloves
- 1 tbsp cornstarch
- 14 oz chicken broth
- 2 tbsp lemon juice
- ¼ tsp salt
- 1 cup frozen peas
- 1 ½ cups uncooked instant rice

Directions:

1. Add butter into the skillet and cook over medium-high flame.

2. Then, add garlic, carrot, chicken, and onion and cook for 5–7 minutes.

3. Combine salt, lemon juice, broth, and cornstarch in a bowl, then add to the skillet. Let cook and stir for 1–2 minutes.

4. Add peas and rice and stir well.

5. When done, remove from flame.

6. Let stand for 5 minutes.

7. Serve and enjoy!

Per serving: Calories: 370 kcal; Fat: 9 g; Carbs: 41 g; Protein: 29 g; Sugar: 1 g

30.   Spring Soup with Gourmet Grains

Preparation time: 10 minutes

Cooking time: 25 minutes

Servings: 2

Ingredients:

- 2-tbsp olive oil
- 1-pc small onion, diced
- 6-cups chicken broth
- 1-bay leaf
- ½-cup of fresh dill, chopped (divided)
- 1/3 cup Italian or Arborio whole grain rice
- 1-cup asparagus, chopped
- 1-cup carrots, diced
- 1½-cups cooked chicken, de-boned and diced or shredded
- ½-lemon, juice
- 1-pc large egg
- 2-tbsp water
- Kosher salt and fresh pepper to taste
- Fresh chives, minced garnish

Directions:

1. Heat olive oil and sauté onions for 5 minutes in a large stockpot placed over medium heat. Pour in chicken broth.

2. Add bay leaf and half of the dill. Bring to a boil.

3. Add rice and turn the heat to medium-low. Simmer for 10 minutes.

4. Add asparagus and carrots. Cook 15 minutes 'til vegetables are tender and rice cooks through.

5. Add cooked shredded chicken. Continue simmering over low heat.

6. In the meantime, combine lemon juice and egg with water in a mixing bowl.

7. Take ½-cup of simmering stock and pour it on the lemon-egg mixture, whisking to prevent eggs from curdling.

8. Pour lemon-egg broth into the stockpot, still whisking. Soon as the soup thickens, turn off the heat.

9. Remove the bay leaf, and discard. Add remaining dill, salt, and pepper.

10. To serve, ladle creamy soup in bowls and garnish with minced chives.

Per serving: Calories: 253 kcal; Fat: 8 g; Carbs: 20 g; Protein: 26 g; Sugar: 1 g

31.   Green Beans Greek Style

Preparation time: 5 minutes

Cooking time: 8 minutes

Servings: 2-3

Ingredients:

- 1 cup - Tomato Bouillon Soup
- 2 cups - Green beans
- 8 ounces - Water
- 1 tsp - Onion powder
- 1 tsp - Oregano
- 1 tsp - Garlic powder
- Parsley dash

Directions:

1. In a large saucepan, pour water.

2. Add tomato soup to the water.

3. Now add all ingredients to the saucepan.

4. Cover pan and cook 15 minutes until beans become tender.

5. Serve hot as a side dish.

Per serving: Calories: 134 kcal; Fat: 2 g; Carbs: 32 g; Protein: 12 g; Sugar: 1 g

32. Maple Rice

Preparation time: 20 minutes, plus overnight soaking

Cooking time: 5 minutes

Servings: 4

Ingredients:

- Rice 250g
- Maple syrup 2 tsp
- Water 500 ml

Directions:

1. Toast rice in a pan lightly and soak overnight in 250ml water

2. Add maple syrup, rice, and 250ml water to the blender and blend till smooth.

3. Strain and discard puree

4. Shake bee serving

Per serving: Calories: 33 kcal; Fat: 1 g; Carbs: 8 g; Protein: 1 g; Sugar: 1 g

33. Herbed Harvest Rice

Preparation time: 15 minutes, plus 8 hours to soak

Cooking time: 3 hours on high

Servings: 2

Ingredients:

- 2 cups brown rice, soaked in water overnight, drained and rinsed
- ½ small onion, chopped
- 4 cups vegetable broth
- 2 tablespoons extra-virgin olive oil
- ½ teaspoon dried thyme leaves
- ½ teaspoon garlic powder
- ½ cup cooked sliced mushrooms
- ½ cup dried cranberries
- ½ cup toasted pecans

Directions:

1. In your slow cooker, combine rice, onion, broth, olive oil, thyme, and garlic powder. Stir well.

2. Cover the cooker and set it to high. Cook for 3 hours.

3. Stir in mushrooms, cranberries, and pecans, and serve.

Per serving: Calories: 546 kcal; Fat: 20 g; Carbs: 88 g; Protein: 10 g; Sugar: 14 g

34. Wild Rice with Spicy Chickpeas

Preparation time: 15 minutes

Cooking time: 60 minutes

Servings: 6-7

Ingredients:

- 1 cup basmati rice
- 1 cup wild rice
- Salt & pepper to taste
- 4tbsp Olive oil
- 1tbsp Garlic powder
- 2tsp cumin powder
- ¼ Cup sunflower oil
- 3 cups chickpeas
- 1tsp Flour
- 1tsp Curry powder
- 3tsp Paprika powder
- 1tsp Dill
- 3tbsp parsley (chopped)
- 1 medium onion (thinly sliced)
- 2 Cups currants

Directions:

1. For cooking wild rice, fill the half pot with water and bring it to a boil. Put rice and let it simmer for 40 minutes.

2. Heat olive oil, add cumin powder, salt, and water and boil. Add basmati rice and cook for 20 minutes.

3. Leave rice cooking and prepare spicy chickpeas. Heat 2 tbsp. of olive oil in a pan and toss chickpeas, garlic powder, salt & pepper, cumin, and paprika powder.

4. In a pan, cook onion with sunflower oil until golden brown and add flour.

5. Mix flour and onion with your hands.

6. For serving, place both types of rice in a bowl with spicy chickpeas and fry the onion. Garnish it with parsley and herbs.

Per serving: Calories: 647 kcal; Fat: 26 g; Carbs: 88 g; Protein: 25 g; Sugar: 1 g

35.   Fried Rice with Kale

Preparation time: 10 minutes

Cooking time: 12 minutes

Servings: 4

Ingredients:

- 2 tbsp. olive oil
- 8 oz. Tofu,
- 6 Scallion,
- 2 cups Kale,
- 3 cups cooked brown rice
- ¼ cup Stir fry sauce

Directions:

1. Warm olive oil in a huge skillet on medium-high heat until it shimmers.

2. Add tofu, scallions, and kale. Cook for 5 to 7 minutes, frequently stirring, until vegetables are soft.

3. Add brown rice and stir-fry sauce. Cook for 3-5 minutes, occasionally stirring, until heated through.

Per serving: Calories: 301 kcal; Fat: 11 g; Carbs: 36 g; Protein: 47 g; Sugar: 1 g

36.   Bean Enchiladas

Preparation time: 20 minutes

Cooking time: 30 minutes

Servings: 4

Ingredients:

- Red beans
- low-fat cheddar cheese
- onion
- black olives
- tomato sauce
- garlic salt
- whole wheat tortillas

Directions:

1. Preheat oven to 350F degrees. In a bowl, combine one cup of tomato sauce, garlic salt, onions, olives, cheese, and mashed beans.

2. Place 1/3 cup of beans along the center of each tortilla. Place enchiladas in the baking dish after it has been rolled.

3. Place tomato sauce on top of already filled tortillas. If desired, sprinkle with more cheese.

4. Bake for 20 minutes or until thoroughly heated.

Per serving: Calories: 231 kcal; Fat: 2 g; Carbs: 13 g; Protein: 12 g; Sugar: 2 g

37.   Spanish Rice

Preparation time: 15 minutes or fewer

Cooking time: 5-6 hours on low

Servings: 2

Ingredients:

- 2 cups white rice
- 2 cups vegetable broth
- 2 tablespoons extra-virgin olive oil
- 1 (14.5-ounce) can of crushed tomatoes
- 1 (4-ounce) can Hatch green chilis
- ½ medium onion, diced
- 1 teaspoon salt
- ½ teaspoon ground cumin
- ½ teaspoon garlic powder
- ½ teaspoon chili powder
- ½ teaspoon dried oregano
- Pepper

Directions:

1. In your slow cooker, combine rice, broth, olive oil, tomatoes, chilis, onion, salt, cumin, garlic powder, chili powder, and oregano, and season with pepper.

2. Cover the cooker and set it to low. Cook for 5 - 6 hours, fluff, and serve.

Per serving: Calories: 406 kcal; Fat: 7 g; Carbs: 79 g; Protein: 8 g; Sugar: 5 g

38.   Spiced Soup with Lentils & Legumes

Preparation time: 15 minutes

Cooking time: 35 minutes

Servings: 2

Ingredients:

- 2 tbsp extra-virgin olive oil
- 2-cloves garlic, minced
- 4-pcs large celery stalks, diced
- 2 pcs large onions, diced
- 6-cups water
- 1-tsp cumin
- ¾-tsp turmeric
- ½-tsp cinnamon
- ½-tsp fresh ginger, grated
- 1-cup dried lentils, rinsed and sorted
- 1-16-oz. can chickpeas (garbanzo beans), drained and rinsed
- 3 pcs ripe tomatoes, cubed
- ½-lemon, juice
- ½ cup fresh cilantro or parsley, chopped
- Salt

Directions:

1. Heat olive oil and sauté garlic, celery, and onion for 5 minutes in a large stockpot placed over medium heat.

2. Pour in water. Add spices and lentils. Cover stockpot and simmer for 40 minutes until lentils are tender.

3. Add chickpeas and tomatoes. (Pour more water and additional spices, if desired.) Simmer for 15 minutes over low heat.

4. Pour in lemon juice and stir the soup. Add cilantro or parsley and salt to taste.

Per serving: Calories: 123 kcal; Fat: 3 g; Carbs: 19 g; Protein: 5 g; Sugar: 1 g

39.   Italian Bean Soup

Preparation time: 15 minutes

Cooking time: 15 minutes

Servings: 2

Ingredients:

- tbsp virgin olive oil
- onion (diced)
- garlic cloves (minced)
- cups tomato sauce (homemade or 1 can of low-sodium organic canned tomato sauce)
- cups cooked cannellini beans (or 24 ounces of canned beans that have been drained and rinsed)
- 2tbsp basil (dried)
- ½ tsp oregano
- ¼ tsp pepper

Directions:

1. Take a large soup or stockpot and place it on the stove. Turn Heat to medium-high and pour in virgin olive oil.

2. Allow the oil to heat slightly before adding diced onions to the pot. Saute for 3 minutes and adds garlic. Let flavors come together.

3. Add cannellini beans, basil, oregano, and pepper to the pot. Stir everything together and pour over tomato sauce.

4. Allow sauce to come to a steady simmer. Reduce heat to medium-low. Cover pot so flavors can simmer together for 5 minutes.

5. Uncover the pot and allow the aroma to fill the kitchen. Take a ladle and fill soup bowls! Grab a soup spoon and enjoy

Per serving: Calories: 164 kcal; Fat: 1 g; Carbs: 26 g; Protein: 8 g; Sugar: 1 g

40.   Coconutty Brown Rice

Preparation time: 15 minutes, plus 8 hours to soak

Cooking time: 3 hours on high

Servings: 2

Ingredients:

- 2 cups brown rice, soaked in water overnight, drained and rinsed

- 3 cups water
- 1½ cups full-fat coconut milk
- 1 teaspoon salt
- ½ teaspoon ground ginger
- Pepper

Directions:

1. Combine rice, water, coconut milk, salt, and ginger in your slow cooker. Season with pepper and stir to incorporate spices.

2. Cover the cooker and set it to high. Cook for 3 hours and serve.

Per serving: Calories: 479 kcal; Fat: 19 g; Carbs: 73 g; Protein: 9 g; Sugar: 1 g

CHAPTER 3: Salads And Vegetables

41. Greek Chop-Chop Salad

Preparation time: 15 minutes

Cooking time: 0 minutes

Servings: 4-5

Ingredients:

- 1 medium English cucumber, chopped (2 cups)
- 1 cup halved cherry tomatoes
- 1 red bell pepper, seeded and diced
- ½ red onion, diced
- ½ cup pitted Kalamata olives, roughly chopped
- 1 cup crumbled feta cheese
- ½ cup balsamic dressing

Directions:

1. In a large bowl, toss cucumber, tomatoes, bell pepper, onion, olives, and cheese with dressing, and serve.

Per serving: Calories: 179 kcal; Fat: 13 g; Carbs: 10 g; Protein: 4 g; Sugar: 4 g

42. Asian Cabbage Salad

Preparation time: 10 minutes

Cooking time: 0 minutes

Servings: 2-3

Ingredients:

- 1 (14-ounce) package of coleslaw
- 1 red bell pepper, thinly sliced
- 1 large carrot, grated
- ¼ cup diced scallions
- ¼ cup chopped fresh cilantro
- ¼ cup chopped peanuts
- 1/3 cup Spicy Peanut Dressing, plus more if desired

Directions:

1. In a large bowl, combine coleslaw, bell pepper, carrot, scallions, cilantro, and peanuts.

2. Toss with dressing, add more as desired, and serve.

Per serving: Calories: 123 kcal; Fat: 6 g; Carbs: 16 g; Protein: 6 g; Sugar: 6 g

43. Tenderloin Grilled Salad

Preparation time: 10 minutes

Cooking time: 20 minutes

Servings: 5

Ingredients:

- 1 lb. pork tenderloin
- 10 c. mixed salad greens
- 2 oranges, seedless, cut into bite-sized pieces
- 1 tbsp. orange zest, grated

For the Dressing

- 2 tbsps. of cider vinegar
- 2 tbsps. olive oil
- 2 tsps. Dijon mustard
- 1/2 c. juice of an orange
- 2 tsps. honey
- 1/2 tsp. ground pepper

Directions:

1. Bring together all the dressing ingredients in a bowl.

2. Grill each side of the pork covered over medium heat for 9 minutes.

3. Slice after 5 minutes.

4. Slice the tenderloin thinly.

5. Keep the greens on your serving plate.

6. Top with the pork and oranges.

7. Sprinkle nuts (optional).

Per serving: Calories: 211 kcal; Fat: 9 g; Carbs: 13 g; Protein: 20 g; Sugar: 1 g

44. Tomato, Basil, and Cucumber Salad

Preparation time: 15 minutes

Cooking time: 15 minutes

Servings: 2-3

Ingredients:

- 1 large cucumber, seeded and sliced
- 4 medium tomatoes, quartered
- 1 medium red onion, thinly sliced
- ½ cup chopped fresh basil
- 3 tbsps. red wine vinegar
- 1 tbsp extra-virgin olive oil
- ½ tsp Dijon mustard
- ½ tsp pepper

Directions:

1. Mix cucumber, tomatoes, red onion, and basil in a medium bowl.

2. Whisk together vinegar, olive oil, mustard, and pepper in a small bowl.

3. Pour dressing over vegetables, then gently stir until well combined.

4. Cover and chill 30 minutes before serving.

Per serving: Calories: 72 kcal; Fat: 4 g; Carbs: 8 g; Protein: 1 g; Sugar: 4 g

45. Salad Bites

Preparation time: 10 minutes

Cooking time: 8 minutes

Servings: 2-3

Ingredients:

- Bites
- 24 cherry tomatoes
- 12 mozzarella balls
- 12 fresh basil leaves
- Balsamic Glaze
- ½ cup balsamic vinegar
- 2 tbsps. extra-virgin olive oil
- 1 garlic clove, minced
- 1 tsp Italian seasoning

Directions:

To make bites

1. Using 12 toothpicks or short skewers, assemble each with one cherry tomato, mozzarella ball, basil leaf, and tomato.

2. Place on a serving platter or in a large glass storage container that can be sealed.

To make glaze

3. In a small saucepan, bring the balsamic to a simmer. Simmer for 15 minutes or until syrupy. Set aside to cool and thicken.

4. Whisk olive oil, garlic, Italian seasoning, and cooled vinegar in a small bowl.

5. Drizzle olive oil and balsamic glaze over the skewers. Serve immediately, or keep it in the refrigerator as a tasty snack.

Per serving: Calories: 39 kcal; Fat: 3 g; Carbs: 3 g; Protein: 1 g; Sugar: 0 g

46. Mango and Jicama Salad

Preparation time: 15 minutes

Cooking time: 5 minutes

Servings: 8

Ingredients:

- 1 jicama, peeled
- 1 mango, peeled
- 1 tsp. ginger root, minced
- 1/3 c. chives, minced
- 1/2 c. cilantro, chopped
- 1/4 c. canola oil
- 1/2 c. white wine vinegar
- 2 tbsps. of lime juice
- 1/4 c. honey
- 1/8 tsp. pepper
- 1/4 tsp. salt

Directions:

1. Whisk together the vinegar, honey, canola oil, gingerroot, paper, and salt.

2. Cut the mango and jicama into matchsticks.

3. Keep it in a bowl.

4. Now toss with the lime juice.

5. Add the dressing and herbs. Combine well by tossing.

Per serving: Calories: 143 kcal; Fat: 7 g; Carbs: 20 g; Protein: 1 g; Sugar: 2 g

47.   Roasted Garden Vegetables

Preparation time: 5 minutes

Cooking time: 15 minutes

Servings: 2-3

Ingredients:

- 1 medium bell pepper, cut into strips
- 1 small onion, halved & sliced
- 1 small zucchini, sliced in rounds
- 1-pint grape tomatoes
- 2 tbsps. extra-virgin olive oil
- Salt
- Pepper

Directions:

1. Preheat oven to 400°F.

2. Arrange vegetables lying flat on baking sheets.

3. Evenly pour olive oil over vegetables and gently toss to coat, using a spoon or hands. Add salt and pepper to taste.

4. Roast 20 to 30 minutes until soft and lightly charred, stirring halfway through, and serve.

Per serving: Calories: 75 kcal; Fat: 5 g; Carbs: 8 g; Protein: 0 g; Sugar: 4 g

48.   Roasted Beet Salad

Preparation time: 10 minutes

Cooking time: 10 minutes

Servings: 4

Ingredients:

- 2 beets
- 1 garlic clove, minced
- 2 tbsps. walnuts, chopped and toasted
- 1 c. fennel bulb, sliced
- 3 tbsps. balsamic vinegar
- 1 tsp. Dijon mustard
- 1 tbsp. honey
- 3 tbsps. olive oil
- 1/4 tsp. pepper
- 1/4 tsp. salt
- 3 tbsps. water

Directions:

1. Scrub the beets. Trim the tops to 1 in.

2. Wrap in foil and keep on a baking sheet.

3. Bake until tender. Take off the foil.

4. Cover. Microwave for 5 minutes. Drain off.

5. Now peel the beets. Cut into small wedges.

6. Arrange the fennel and beets on four salad plates.

7. Sprinkle nuts.

8. Whisk the honey, mustard, vinegar, water, garlic, pepper, and salt.

9. Whisk in oil gradually.

10. Drizzle over the salad.

Per serving: Calories: 273 kcal; Fat: 13 g; Carbs: 37 g; Protein: 5 g; Sugar: 1 g

49.   Basil Avocado Pasta Salad

Preparation time: 5 minutes

Cooking time: 0 minutes

Servings: 1

Ingredients:

- 1 avocado, chopped
- 1 c. fresh basil, chopped
- 1 pint cherry tomatoes halved
- 1 tbsp. key lime juice
- 1 tsp. agave syrup
- 1/4 c. olive oil
- 4 c. cooked spelt-pasta
- Sea salt, to taste

Directions:

1. Place the cooked pasta in a big bowl. Add the avocado, basil, and tomatoes and mix until thoroughly blended.

2. Whisk the oil, lime juice, agave syrup, and sea salt in a deep mixing pot. Toss over the pasta, then stir to blend.

Per serving: Calories: 491 kcal; Fat: 26 g; Carbs: 50 g; Protein: 15 g; Sugar: 3 g

50.   Grapefruit-Pomegranate Salad

Preparation time: 10 minutes

Cooking time: 0 minutes

Servings: 6

Ingredients:

- 2 ruby red grapefruits
- 3 ounces Parmesan cheese
- 1 pomegranate
- 6 cups mesclun leaves
- ¼ cup Basic Vegetable Stock

Directions:

1. Peel grapefruit using a knife, and take off all pith. (white layer under the skin).

2. Cut out every section with the knife, and ensure that no pith remains. Shave Parmesan using a vegetable peeler to curl.

3. Peel pomegranate using a paring knife; take off berries/seeds.

4. Toss mesclun greens in stock.

5. To serve, mound greens on plates and arrange grapefruit sections, cheese, and pomegranate on top.

Per serving: Calories: 84 kcal; Fat: 2 g; Carbs: 14 g; Protein: 4 g; Sugar: 3 g

51.   Thai Quinoa Salad

Preparation time: 10 minutes

Cooking time: 0 minutes

Servings: 1–2

Ingredients:

- For the Dressing
- 1 tbsp. sesame seed
- 1 tsp. chopped garlic
- 1 tsp. lemon, fresh juice
- 3 tsp. apple cider vinegar
- 2 tsp. tamari, gluten-free.
- 1/4 c of tahini (sesame butter)
- 1 pitted date
- 1/2 tsp. salt
- 1/2 tsp. toasted sesame oil
- For the Salad
- 1 c of quinoa, steamed
- 1 big handful of arugulas
- 1 tomato cut into pieces
- 1/4 of the red onion, diced

Directions:

1. Add filtered water and all the ingredients for the dressing into a small blender. Mix.

2. Steam the quinoa in a steamer or a rice pan, then set aside.

3. Combine the quinoa, the arugula, the sliced tomatoes, and the red onion diced on a serving plate or bowl, add the Thai dressing and serve with a spoon.

Per serving: Calories: 100 kcal; Fat: 9 g; Carbs: 12 g; Protein: 16 g; Sugar: 7 g

52.   Roasted Root Vegetables

Preparation time: 15 minutes

Cooking time: 45 minutes

Servings: 2-3

Ingredients:

- Nonstick cooking spray
- 2 medium red beets, peeled
- 2 large parsnips, peeled
- 2 large carrots, peeled
- 1 medium butternut squash
- 1 medium red onion
- 2 tbsps. extra-virgin olive oil
- 4 tsps. minced garlic
- 2 tsps. dried thyme

Directions:

1. Preheat oven to 425°F. Spray a baking sheet with cooking spray.

2. Roughly chop beets, parsnips, carrots, and butternut squash into 1-inch pieces. Cut onion in half and each half into four large chunks.

3. Arrange vegetables in single, even layers on the baking sheet, and sprinkle with olive oil, garlic, and thyme. Use a spoon to mix vegetables to coat them with oil and seasonings.

4. Roast for 45 minutes, stirring vegetables every 15 minutes, until all vegetables are tender.

5. Serve immediately.

Per serving: Calories: 68 kcal; Fat: 3 g; Carbs: 11 g; Protein: 1 g; Sugar: 5 g

53. Dandelion Strawberry Salad

Preparation time: 15 minutes

Cooking time: 10 minutes

Servings: 2

Ingredients:

- 2 tbsp. grapeseed oil
- 1 medium red onion, sliced
- 10 ripe strawberries, sliced
- 2 tbsp. key lime juice
- 4 c. dandelion greens
- Sea salt to taste

Directions:

1. First, warm grapeseed oil in a 12-in. non-stick frying pan over medium heat. Add some sliced onions and a small pinch of sea salt. Cook until the onions are soft, lightly brown, and reduced to about 1/3 of raw volume, stirring frequently.

2. Then toss the strawberry slices in a tiny bowl with 1 tsp of key lime juice. Rinse the dandelion greens and, if you prefer, slice them into bite-size chunks.

3. When it's about to be cooked, put the remaining key lime juice into the saucepan and cook until it has thickened to coat the onions for 1–2 minutes. Remove the onions from the heat.

4. Combine the vegetables, onions, and strawberries with all their juices in a salad bowl. Sprinkle with sea salt.

Per serving: Calories: 151 kcal; Fat: 13 g; Carbs: 2 g; Protein: 7 g; Sugar: 10 g

54. French Style Potato Salad

Preparation time: 10 minutes

Cooking time: 0 minutes

Servings: 4

Ingredients:

Potatoes

- 2 lbs. baby yellow potatoes, boiled, peeled, and diced
- 1 pinch salt and pepper
- 1 tbsp apple cider vinegar
- 1 cup green onion, diced
- ¼ cup fresh parsley, chopped

Dressing

- 2½ tbsps. brown mustard
- 3 cloves garlic, minced
- ¼ tsp salt and pepper
- 3 tbsps. red wine vinegar
- 1 tbsp apple cider vinegar
- 3 tbsps. olive oil
- ¼ cup dill, chopped

Directions:

1. Combine all dressing ingredients in a salad bowl.

2. In a salad bowl, toss vegetables, seasonings, and dressing.

3. Mix well and refrigerate to chill.

4. Serve.

Per serving: Calories: 197 kcal; Fat: 4 g; Carbs: 31 g; Protein: 11 g; Sugar: 3 g

55. Loaded Kale Salad

Preparation time: 10 minutes

Cooking time: 0 minutes

Servings: 4

Ingredients:

Quinoa

- ¾ cups quinoa, cooked and drained

Vegetables

- 4 large carrots, halved and chopped
- 1 whole beet, sliced
- 2 tbsps. water
- 1 pinch salt
- ½ tsp curry powder
- 8 cups kale, chopped
- ½ cups cherry tomatoes, chopped

- 1 ripe avocado, cubed
- ¼ cup hemp seeds
- ½ cup sprouts

Dressing

- ⅓ cup tahini
- 3 tbsps. lemon juice
- 1-2 tbsps. maple syrup
- 1 pinch salt
- ¼ cup water

Directions:

1. Combine all dressing ingredients in a small bowl.
2. In a salad bowl, toss in vegetables, quinoa, and dressing.
3. Mix well and refrigerate to chill.
4. Serve.

Per serving: Calories: 72 kcal; Fat: 15 g; Carbs: 28 g; Protein: 8 g; Sugar: 2 g

56. Pureed Classic Egg Salad

Preparation time: 5 minutes

Cooking time: 2 minutes

Servings: 2-3

Ingredients:

- 2 - Eggs, hard-boiled
- 1 tbsp - Low-fat mayonnaise
- 1 tbsp – Greek yogurt, plain

Directions:

1. Cut boiled eggs into even portions.
2. Put slices of eggs in a food mixer and chop them.
3. Add salt, mayonnaise, and Greek yogurt as seasonings to eggs
4. Mix finely as far as the egg salad becomes smooth.

Per serving: Calories: 134 kcal; Fat: 2 g; Carbs: 12 g; Protein: 6 g; Sugar: 1 g

57. French Broccoli Salad

Preparation time: 10 minutes,

Cooking time: 10 minutes;

Servings: 10

Ingredients:

- 8 c. broccoli florets
- 3 strips of bacon, cooked and crumbled
- 1/4 c. sunflower kernels
- 1 bunch of green onion, sliced
- 3 tbsps. seasoned rice vinegar
- 3 tbsps. canola oil
- 1/2 c. dried cranberries

Directions:

1. Combine the green onion, cranberries, and broccoli in a bowl.
2. Whisk the vinegar and oil in another bowl. Blend well.
3. Now drizzle over the broccoli mix.
4. Coat well by tossing.
5. Sprinkle bacon and sunflower kernels before serving.

Per serving: Calories: 121 kcal; Fat: 7 g; Carbs: 14 g; Protein: 3 g; Sugar: 1 g

58. Barley Veggie Salad

Preparation time: 10 minutes,

Cooking time: 20 minutes;

Servings: 6

Ingredients:

- 1 tomato, seeded and chopped
- 2 tbsps. parsley, minced
- 1 yellow pepper, chopped
- 1 tbsp. basil, minced
- 1/4 c. almonds, toasted
- 1–1/4 c. vegetable broth
- 1 c. barley
- 1 tbsp. lemon juice
- 2 tbsps. of white wine vinegar
- 3 tbsps. olive oil
- 1/4 tsp. pepper

- 1/2 tsp. salt
- 1 c of water

Directions:

1. Boil the broth, barley, and water in a saucepan.

2. Reduce the heat. Cover and let it simmer for 10 minutes.

3. Take out from the heat.

4. In the meantime, bring together the parsley, yellow pepper, and tomato in a bowl.

5. Stir the barley in.

6. Whisk the vinegar, oil, basil, lemon juice, water, pepper, and salt in a bowl.

7. Pour this over your barley mix. Toss to coat well.

8. Stir the almonds before serving.

Per serving: Calories: 211 kcal; Fat: 10 g; Carbs: 27 g; Protein: 6 g; Sugar: 0 g

59.   Nutty and Fruity Garden Salad

Preparation time: 10 minutes

Cooking time: 0 minutes

Servings: 2

Ingredients:

- 6 cups baby spinach
- ½ cup chopped walnuts, toasted
- 1 ripe red pear, sliced
- 1 ripe persimmon, sliced
- 1 tsp garlic minced
- 1 shallot, minced
- 1 tbsp extra-virgin olive oil
- 2 tbsps. fresh lemon juice
- 1 tsp wholegrain mustard

Directions:

1. Mix well garlic, oil, shallot, mustard, and lemon juice

2. Add spinach, pear, and persimmon. Toss to coat well.

3. To serve, garnish with chopped pecans.

Per serving: Calories: 332 kcal; Fat: 21 g; Carbs: 37 g; Protein: 7 g; Sugar: 1 g

60.   Calico Salad

Preparation time: 15 minutes

Cooking time: 5 minutes

Servings: 14

Ingredients:

- 1–1/2 c. kernel corn, cooked
- 1/2 c. green pepper, diced
- 1/2 c. red onion, chopped
- 1 c. carrot, shredded
- 1/2 c. olive oil
- 1/4 c. vinegar
- 1–1/2 tsps. chili powder
- 1 tsp. salt
- Dash of hot pepper sauce

Directions:

1. Keep all the ingredients for the store cupboard together in a jar.

2. Close it and shake it well.

3. Combine with carrot, green pepper, onion, and corn in your salad bowl.

4. Pour the dressing over.

5. Now toss lightly.

Per serving: Calories: 146 kcal; Fat: 9 g; Carbs: 17 g; Protein: 2 g; Sugar: 0 g

CHAPTER 4: Meat

61.   Barbecue Beef Brisket

Preparation time: 25 minutes

Cooking time: 10 hours

Servings: 10

Ingredients:

- 4 lb. beef brisket (boneless), trimmed and sliced
- 1 bay leaf
- 2 onions, sliced into rings
- 1/2 tsp. dried thyme, crushed
- 1/4 c. chili sauce
- 1 garlic clove, minced
- Salt and pepper to taste
- 2 tbsps. cornstarch
- 2 tbsps. cold water

Directions:

1. Put the meat in a slow cooker.
2. Add the bay leaf and onion.
3. Mix the thyme, chili sauce, salt, pepper, and sugar in a bowl.
4. Pour the sauce over the meat.
5. Mix well.
6. Seal the pot and cook on low heat for 10 hours.
7. Discard the bay leaf.
8. Pour the cooking liquid into a pan.
9. Add the mixed water and cornstarch.
10. Simmer until the sauce has thickened.
11. Pour the sauce over the meat.

Per serving: Calories: 182 kcal; Fat: 6 g; Carbs: 83 g; Protein: 20 g; Sugar: 4 g

62.   Italian Beef

Preparation time: 20 minutes

Cooking time: 1 hour and 20 minutes

Servings: 4

Ingredients:

- Cooking spray
- 1 lb. beef round steak, trimmed and sliced
- 1 c. onion, chopped
- 2 cloves garlic, minced
- 1 c. green bell pepper, chopped
- 1/2 c. celery, chopped
- 2 c. mushrooms, sliced
- 14 1/2 oz. canned diced tomatoes
- 1/2 tsp. dried basil
- 1/4 tsp. dried oregano
- 1/8 tsp. crushed red pepper
- 2 tbsps. Parmesan cheese, grated

Directions:

1. Spray oil on the pan over medium heat.
2. Cook the meat until brown on both sides.
3. Transfer the meat to a plate.
4. Add the onion, garlic, bell pepper, celery, and mushroom to the pan.
5. Cook until tender.
6. Add the tomatoes, herbs, and pepper.
7. Put the meat back into the pan.
8. Simmer while covered for 1 hour and 15 minutes.
9. Stir occasionally.
10. Sprinkle Parmesan cheese on top of the dish before serving.

Per serving: Calories: 213 kcal; Fat: 4 g; Carbs: 11 g; Protein: 30 g; Sugar: 6 g

63.   Hot & Spicy Shredded Chicken

Preparation time: 1 hour

Cooking time: 25 minutes

Servings: 2

Ingredients:

- 1 ½ pound boneless and skinless Chicken Breast
- 2 cups diced Tomatoes
- ½ tsp Oregano
- 2 Green Chilies, seeded and chopped
- ½ tsp Paprika
- 2 tbsp Coconut Sugar

- ½ cup Salsa
- 1 tsp Cumin
- 2 tbsp Olive Oil

Directions:

1. In a small bowl, combine the oil with all of the spices.
2. Rub chicken breast with the spicy marinade.
3. Place meat in your Instant Pot.
4. Add diced tomatoes.
5. Close the lid and cook for 25 minutes
6. Transfer chicken to a cutting board, then shred it.
7. Return shredded meat to the Instant Pot.
8. Choose the "SLOW COOK" setting and cook for 30 more minutes.

Per serving: Calories: 307 kcal; Fat: 10 g; Carbs: 12 g; Protein: 38 g; Sugar: 2 g

64. Creamy Turkey and Mushrooms

Preparation time: 40 minutes

Cooking time: 26 minutes

Servings: 2

Ingredients:

- 20 ounces of Turkey Breasts, boneless and skinless
- 6 ounces White Button Mushrooms, sliced
- 3 tbsp chopped Shallots
- ½ tsp dried Thyme
- 1/3 cup dry White Wine
- 2/3 cup Chicken Stock
- 1 Garlic Clove, minced
- 2 tbsp Olive Oil
- 3 tbsp Heavy Cream
- 1 ½ tbsp Cornstarch
- Salt and Pepper, to taste

Directions:

1. Tie turkey breast with a kitchen string horizontally, leaving approximately 2 inches apart.
2. Season meat with salt and pepper.

3. Heat half of the olive oil in your Instant Pot on SAUTÉ mode.
4. Add turkey and brown it for about 3 minutes on each side. Transfer to a plate.
5. Add remaining oil, followed by shallots, thyme, garlic, and mushrooms and cook for 5 minutes or until translucent.
6. Add white wine, then scrape up brown bits from the bottom.
7. When the alcohol evaporates, return the turkey to the pressure cooker and add chicken broth.
8. Close the lid with the steam vents off and cook for 20 minutes on MANUAL.
9. Combine heavy cream & cornstarch in a small bowl.
10. Carefully open the lid and stir in the mixture.
11. Bring sauce to a boil, then turn the cooker off.
12. Slice turkey in half and serve topped with creamy mushroom sauce.

Per serving: Calories: 192 kcal; Fat: 12 g; Carbs: 5 g; Protein: 15 g; Sugar: 5 g

65. Rosemary Lamb

Preparation time: 15 minutes

Cooking time: 2 hours

Servings: 14

Ingredients:

- Salt and pepper to taste
- 2 tsps. fresh rosemary, snipped
- 5 lb. whole leg of lamb, trimmed and cut with slits on all sides
- 3 cloves garlic, slivered
- 1 c. water

Directions:

1. Preheat your oven to 375 °F.
2. Mix salt, pepper, and rosemary in a bowl.
3. Sprinkle the mixture all over the lamb.
4. Insert slivers of garlic into the slits.
5. Put the lamb in a roasting pan.
6. Add water to the pan.
7. Roast for 2 hours.

Per serving: Calories: 136 kcal; Fat: 4 g; Carbs: 21 g; Protein: 23 g; Sugar: 2 g

66. Slow Cooker Chicken

Preparation time: 10 minutes

Cooking time: 4-6 hours

Servings: 2

Ingredients:

- 4 lb. whole chicken, skin and fat removed
- 1 tsp black pepper
- 1/2 medium-sized onion, quartered
- 1 rib celery, cut into three equal sizes

Directions:

1. Sprinkle half of the pepper over the chicken and another half inside.
2. Place celery and onion inside the cavity and leave for 5-10 minutes.
3. Place peppered whole chicken in a slow cooker, ensuring the breast side faces down.
4. Cook on high for 4-6 hours or until fully cooked.
5. Remove extra chicken skin and discard.

Per serving: Calories: 159 kcal; Fat: 7 g; Carbs: 1 g; Protein: 23 g; Sugar: 2 g

67. Sesame Pork with Mustard Sauce

Preparation time: 25 minutes

Cooking time: 25 minutes

Servings: 4

Ingredients:

- 2 tbsps. low-sodium teriyaki sauce
- 1/4 c. chili sauce
- 2 cloves garlic, minced
- 2 tsps. ginger, grated
- 2 pork tenderloins
- 2 tsps. sesame seeds
- 1/4 c. low-fat sour cream
- 1 tsp. Dijon mustard
- Salt to taste
- 1 scallion, chopped

Directions:

1. Preheat your oven to 425 °F.
2. Mix the teriyaki sauce, chili sauce, garlic, and ginger.
3. Put the pork in a roasting pan.
4. Brush the sauce on both sides of the pork.
5. Bake in the oven for 15 minutes.
6. Brush with more sauce.
7. Top with sesame seeds.
8. Roast for 10 more minutes.
9. Mix the rest of the ingredients.
10. Serve the pork with mustard sauce.

Per serving: Calories: 135 kcal; Fat: 3 g; Carbs: 7 g; Protein: 20 g; Sugar: 15 g

68. Mediterranean Lamb Meatballs

Preparation time: 10 minutes

Cooking time: 20 minutes

Servings: 8

Ingredients:

- 12 oz. roasted red peppers
- 1 1/2 c. whole wheat breadcrumbs
- 2 eggs, beaten
- 1/3 c. tomato sauce
- 1/2 c. fresh basil
- 1/4 c. parsley, snipped
- Salt and pepper to taste
- 2 lb. lean ground lamb

Directions:

1. Preheat your oven to 350 °F.
2. In a bowl, mix all the ingredients and then form them into meatballs.
3. Put the meatballs on a baking pan.
4. Bake in the oven for 20 minutes.

Per serving: Calories: 94 kcal; Fat: 3 g; Carbs: 2 g; Protein: 5 g; Sugar: 0 g

69. Teriyaki Chicken Under Pressure

Preparation time: 25 minutes

Cooking time: 20 minutes

Servings: 2

Ingredients:

- 1 cup Chicken Broth
- 2 tbsp ground Ginger
- 1 tsp Pepper
- 3 pounds Boneless and Skinless Chicken Thighs
- ¼ cup Apple Cider Vinegar
- ¾ cup low-sodium Soy Sauce
- 20 ounces canned Pineapple, crushed
- 2 tbsp Garlic Powder

Directions:

1. Place chicken in your Instant Pot.

2. Combine all of the remaining ingredients in a bowl.

3. Pour sauce over the meat.

4. Seal the lid, select MANUAL and cook for 20 minutes on high pressure.

5. Once cooking is complete, select Cancel and perform a quick release.

6. Serve and enjoy.

Per serving: Calories: 352 kcal; Fat: 11 g; Carbs: 31 g; Protein: 31 g; Sugar: 2 g

70. Chicken with Apples and Potatoes

Preparation time: 10 minutes

Cooking time: 5-7 hours on Low

Servings: 2

Ingredients:

- 1 pound of potatoes, quartered
- 1 small onion, sliced
- 1 pound of apples, sliced and divided
- 1½ pounds skinless chicken legs or thighs
- ⅓ Cup honey
- ¼ cup apple cider vinegar

- 2 tablespoons low- Sugar: 1g Sodium soy sauce (or tamari if gluten-free)
- ½ teaspoon ground cinnamon
- ¼ teaspoon ground cumin

Directions:

1. Put potatoes, onion, and about half of the sliced apples in the bottom of the slow cooker. Stir to mix well, and scatter chicken on top.

2. Mix honey, vinegar, soy sauce, cinnamon, and cumin. Pour sauce into the slow cooker, coating all ingredients.

3. Top with remaining apples.

4. Cook on low for 5 - 7 hours and serve.

Per serving: Calories: 434 kcal; Fat: 2 g; Carbs: 61 g; Protein: 43 g; Sugar: 1 g

71. Beef and Asparagus

Preparation time: 15 minutes

Cooking time: 10 minutes

Servings: 4

Ingredients:

- 2 tsps. olive oil
- 1 lb. lean beef sirloin, trimmed and sliced
- 1 carrot, shredded
- Salt and pepper to taste
- 12 oz. asparagus, trimmed and sliced
- 1 tsp. dried herbs de Provence, crushed
- 1/2 c. Marsala
- 1/4 tsp. lemon zest

Directions:

1. Pour oil into a pan over medium heat.

2. Add the beef and carrot.

3. Season with salt and pepper.

4. Cook for 3 minutes.

5. Add the asparagus and herbs.

6. Cook for 2 minutes.

7. Add the Marsala and lemon zest.

8. Cook for 5 minutes, stirring frequently.

Per serving: Calories: 327 kcal; Fat: 7 g; Carbs: 29 g; Protein: 28 g; Sugar: 3 g

72. Roasted Pork and Apples

Preparation time: 15 minutes

Cooking time: 30 minutes

Servings: 4

Ingredients:

- Salt and pepper to taste
- 1 lb. pork tenderloin
- 1 tbsp. canola oil
- 1 onion, sliced into wedges
- 3 cooking apples, sliced into wedges
- 2/3 c. apple cider
- Sprigs fresh sage

Directions:

1. In a bowl, mix salt, pepper, and sage.
2. Season both sides of pork with this mixture.
3. Place a pan over medium heat.
4. Brown both sides.
5. Transfer to a roasting pan.
6. Add the onion on top and around the pork.
7. Drizzle oil on top of the pork and apples.
8. Roast in the oven at 425 °F for 10 minutes.
9. Add the apples and roast for another 15 minutes.
10. In a pan, boil the apple cider and then simmer for 10 minutes.
11. Pour the apple cider sauce over the pork before serving.

Per serving: Calories: 239 kcal; Fat: 6 g; Carbs: 22 g; Protein: 24 g; Sugar: 16 g

73. Coconut-Curry Chicken

Preparation time: 5 minutes

Cooking time: 4 - 6 hours on Low

Servings: 2

Ingredients:

- 1½ pounds boneless, skinless chicken thighs
- 1 (15-ounce) can of full-fat or light coconut milk
- 3 large carrots, chopped
- 1 onion, chopped
- 4 garlic cloves, minced
- 1 tablespoon curry powder
- 1 teaspoon red pepper flakes
- 1 teaspoon ground ginger
- ½ teaspoon salt
- ½ teaspoon ground coriander
- ¼ teaspoon freshly ground black pepper
- ¼ cup chopped fresh cilantro

Directions:

1. In a slow cooker, Combine chicken, coconut milk, carrots, onion, garlic, curry powder, red pepper flakes, ginger, salt, coriander, and pepper. Stir to mix well.
2. Cook on low for 4 - 6 hours.
3. Garnish with fresh cilantro and serve.

Per serving: Calories: 486 kcal; Fat: 33 g; Carbs: 16 g; Protein: 37 g; Sugar: 24 g

74. Chicken Salad Delight

Preparation time: 30 minutes

Cooking time: 5 minutes

Servings: 2

Ingredients:

- 2 cups diced chicken, fat and skin removed
- 1/2 cup plain, non-fat yogurt
- 1/2 cup celery, finely chopped
- 1/4 tsp black pepper
- 1/4 cup onion, chopped
- 1/4 cup green pepper, chopped
- 1 tsp dried parsley
- 1 tbsp lemon juice
- 1 tsp dry mustard
- 3 cups water

Directions:

1. In a pot filled with 3 cups water, boil chicken over high heat for 3-5 minutes. Drain excess water and let cool.
2. Mix celery, green pepper, onion, and parsley in a large mixing bowl. Add chicken and toss the mixture with lemon juice.
3. In a separate bowl, mix yogurt, black pepper, and mustard.

4. Add dry mixture to chicken mixture and mix thoroughly.

5. Finally, add lemon juice and mix again. Consume immediately.

Per serving: Calories: 181 kcal; Fat: 10 g; Carbs: 3 g; Protein: 18 g; Sugar: 2 g

75.   Cajun Chicken and Potatoes

Preparation time: 10 minutes

Cooking time: 5-7 hours on Low

Servings: 2

Ingredients:

• 2 pounds of skinless chicken

• 1 pound red potatoes or sweet potatoes, quartered

• 1 onion, sliced

• 3 celery stalks, chopped

• 1 bell pepper, seeded and chopped

• ⅓ Cup water

• 2 tablespoons low- Sugar: 1g Sodium soy sauce (or tamari if gluten-free)

• 2 tablespoons apple cider vinegar

• 2 tablespoons Homemade Cajun Blend

• 2 teaspoons honey

• 2 garlic cloves, minced

• 1 teaspoon extra-virgin olive oil

• ¼ teaspoon salt

• ¼ teaspoon freshly ground black pepper

Directions:

1. In a slow cooker, Combine chicken, potatoes, onion, celery, and bell pepper. Stir to mix well.

2. Whisk water, soy sauce, vinegar, Cajun blend, honey, garlic, olive oil, salt, and pepper in an average bowl. Pour sauce over ingredients in the slow cooker.

3. Cook on low for 5 - 7 hours and serve.

Per serving: Calories: 271 kcal; Fat: 6 g; Carbs: 18 g; Protein: 36 g; Sugar: 2 g

CHAPTER 5: Fish And Seafood

76.   Simple Salmon with Eggs

Preparation time: 2 minutes

Cooking time: 5 minutes

Servings: 3

Ingredients:

- 1 lb. Salmon, cooked, mashed
- 2 Eggs, whisked
- 2 Onions, chopped
- 2 stalks of celery, chopped
- 1 cup Parsley, chopped
- 1 tbsp. Olive oil
- Salt and Pepper, to taste

Directions:

1. Mix salmon, celery, onion, parsley, and salt and pepper, in a bowl. Then in 6 patties, 1-inch-thick and dip in whisked eggs. Heat oil in Instant pot on Sauté mode.

2. Add patties to the pot, cook on both sides for 5 minutes and transfer to a plate. Allow to cool and serve.

Per serving: Calories: 331 kcal; Fat: 16 g; Carbs: 5 g; Protein: 38 g; Sugar: 1 g

77.   Shrimp with Spicy Spinach

Preparation time: 10 minutes

Cooking time: 15 minutes

Servings: 4

Ingredients:

- ¼ cup Extra Olive Oil. divided
- 1½ Pound Peeled Shrimp
- 1 tsp. Sea Salt, divided
- 4 cups fresh baby spinach
- 6 Garlic cloves, minced
- ½ cup Freshly Squeezed Orange Juice
- 1 tbsp. Sriracha Sauce
- ⅛ tsp. Pepper

Directions:

1. In a huge nonstick skillet on medium-high heat, heat 2 tbsps. of olive oil until it shimmers.

2. Add shrimp and ½ tsp salt. Cook for 4 minutes, occasionally stirring, until shrimp are pink. Transfer shrimp to a plate, tent with aluminum foil to keep warm, and set aside.

3. Put the skillet back to Heat and heat the remaining 2 tbsps. of olive oil until it shimmers.

4. Add spinach. Cook for 3 minutes, stirring.

5. Add garlic. Cook for 30 seconds, stirring constantly.

6. Mix orange juice, Sriracha, remaining ½ tsp salt, and pepper in a small bowl. Add this to spinach and cook for 3 minutes. Serve shrimp with spinach on the side.

Per serving: Calories: 317 kcal; Fat: 16 g; Carbs: 7 g; Protein: 38 g; Sugar: 3 g

78.   Healthy Halibut Fillets

Preparation time: 5 minutes

Cooking time: 10 minutes

Servings: 2

Ingredients:

- 2 Halibut fillets
- 1 tbsp. Dill
- 1 tbsp. Onion powder
- 1 cup Parsley, chopped
- 2 tbsp. Paprika
- 1 tbsp. Garlic powder
- 1 tbsp. Lemon Pepper
- 2 tbsp. Lemon juice

Directions:

1. Mix lemon juice, lemon pepper, garlic powder, paprika, parsley, dill and onion powder in a bowl. Pour mixture into Instant pot and place halibut fish over it.

2. Seal the lid, press Manual mode, and cook for 10 minutes (high).

Per serving: Calories: 283 kcal; Fat: 16 g; Carbs: 6 g; Protein: 23 g; Sugar: 1 g

79. Cod with Ginger

Preparation time: 10 minutes

Cooking time: 15 minutes

Servings: 4

Ingredients:

- 2 tbsp. Extra Virgin Olive Oil
- 4 (6 oz.) Cod Fillets
- 1 tbsp. Grated fresh ginger
- 1 tsp. Sea Salt, divided
- ¼ tsp. Pepper
- 5 Garlic cloves, minced
- ¼ cup Fresh Cilantro Leaves, chopped

Directions:

1. Heat olive oil in a huge nonstick skillet at medium-high heat until it shimmers.

2. Season cod with ginger, ½ tsp of salt, and pepper. Put it in hot oil, and cook for 4 minutes per side until the fish is opaque. Take the cod from the pan and set it aside on a platter tented with aluminum foil.

3. Put the skillet back to Heat and add garlic. Cook for 30 seconds, stirring constantly.

4. Cook for 5 minutes, stirring occasionally.

5. Stir cilantro over cod.

Per serving: Calories: 41 kcal; Fat: 2 g; Carbs: 33 g; Protein: 50 g; Sugar: 1 g

80. Clean Salmon with Soy Sauce

Preparation time: 10 minutes

Cooking time: 30 minutes

Servings: 2

Ingredients:

- 2 Salmon fillets
- 2 tbsp. Avocado oil
- 2 tbsp. Soy sauce
- 1 tbsp. Garlic powder
- 1 tbsp. fresh Dill to garnish
- Salt and Pepper, to taste

Directions:

1. To make the marinade, thoroughly mix soy sauce, avocado oil, salt, pepper, and garlic powder in a bowl. Dip salmon in mixture and place in refrigerator for 20 minutes.

2. Transfer contents to Instant pot. Seal, set on Manual, and cook for 10 minutes (high). When ready, do a quick release. Serve topped with fresh dill.

Per serving: Calories: 512 kcal; Fat: 21 g; Carbs: 3 g; Protein: 65 g; Sugar: 2 g

81. Lemony Mussels

Preparation time: 5 minutes

Cooking time: 5 minutes

Servings: 4

Ingredients:

- 1 tbsp. extra virgin extra virgin olive oil
- 2 minced garlic cloves
- 2 lbs. scrubbed mussels
- Juice of one lemon

Directions:

1. Put some water in a pot, add mussels, bring to a boil over medium heat, cook 5 minutes, discard unopened mussels and transfer to a bowl.

2. Mix oil with garlic and freshly squeezed lemon juice in a bowl, whisk well, and add over mussels, toss and serve.

3. Enjoy!

Per serving: Calories: 140 kcal; Fat: 4 g; Carbs: 8 g; Protein: 8 g; Sugar: 4 g

82. Mexican Cod Fillets

Preparation time: 10 minutes

Cooking time: 10 minutes

Servings: 3

Ingredients:

- 3 Cod fillets
- 1 Onion, sliced
- 2 cups Cabbage
- Juice from 1 Lemon
- 1 Jalapeno Pepper
- ½ tsp Oregano
- ½ tsp Cumin powder
- ½ tsp Cayenne Pepper

- 2 tbsp. Olive oil
- Salt and Pepper to taste

Directions:

1. Heat oil on Sauté; add onion, cabbage, lemon juice, jalapeño pepper, cayenne pepper, cumin powder, and oregano, and stir to combine. Cook for 8-10 minutes.

2. Season with salt and pepper. Arrange cod fillets in sauce, using a spoon to cover each piece with sauce. Seal the lid and press Manual. Cook for 5 minutes (High).

Per serving: Calories: 306 kcal; Fat: 19 g; Carbs: 7 g; Protein: 21 g; Sugar: 1 g

83.   Salmon and Roasted Peppers

Preparation time: 5 min

Cooking time: 25 min

Servings: 4

Ingredients:

- 1 cup red peppers, cut into strips
- 4 salmon fillets, boneless
- ¼ cup chicken stock
- 2 tbsps. olive oil
- 1 yellow onion, chopped
- 1 tbsp cilantro, chopped
- Pinch of sea salt
- Pinch pepper

Directions:

1. Warm a pan with oil on medium-high heat; add onion and sauté 5 minutes.

2. Put fish and cook for 5 minutes on each side.

3. Add the rest of the ingredients, introduce the pan to the oven, and cook at 390 degrees F for 10 minutes.

4. Divide the mix between plates and serve.

Per serving: Calories: 265 kcal; Fat: 7 g; Carbs: 1 g; Protein: 16 g; Sugar: 1 g

84.   Shrimp and Corn

Preparation time: 5 minutes

Cooking time: 10 minutes

Servings: 4

Ingredients:

- 1-pound shrimp, peeled and deveined
- 2 garlic cloves, minced
- 1 cup corn
- ½ cup veggie stock
- 1 bunch parsley, chopped
- Juice of 1 lime
- 2 tbsps. olive oil
- Pinch of sea salt
- Pinch of pepper

Directions:

1. Warm a pan with oil on medium-high heat; put garlic and corn and sauté 2 minutes.

2. Add shrimp and/or ingredients, toss, cook everything 8 minutes more, divide between plates, and serve.

Per serving: Calories: 343 kcal; Fat: 11 g; Carbs: 34 g; Protein: 29 g; Sugar: 1 g

85.   Sesame-Tuna Skewers

Preparation time: 10 minutes

Cooking time: 15 minutes

Servings: 6

Ingredients:

- 6 oz. cubed thick tuna steaks
- Cooking spray
- ¼ tsp. Pepper.
- ¾ c. sesame seeds
- 1 tsp. Salt
- ½ tsp. Ground ginger.
- 2 tbsps. toasted sesame oil

Directions:

1. Preheat oven to 400°F.

2. Coat the baking tray with cooking spray.

3. Soak skewers in water

4. Mix pepper, ground ginger, salt, and sesame seeds in a small mixing bowl.

5. In a bowl, toss tuna with sesame oil.

6. Press oiled cubes in a sesame seed mixture and put cubes on each skewer.

7. Put skewers on a prepared baking tray and the tray in a preheated oven.

8. Bake for 12 minutes and turn once.

9. Serve and enjoy.

Per serving: Calories: 196 kcal; Fat: 15 g; Carbs: 3 g; Protein: 15 g; Sugar: 1 g

86.   Scallops with Mushroom Special

Preparation time: 15 minutes

Cooking time: 20 minutes

Servings: 2

Ingredients:

- 1 lb. Scallops
- 2 Onions, chopped
- 1 tbsp. Butter
- 2 tbsp. Olive oil
- 1 cup Mushrooms
- Salt and Pepper, to taste
- 1 tbsp. Lemon juice
- ½ cup Whipping Cream
- 1 tbsp. chopped fresh Parsley

Directions:

1. Heat oil on Sauté. Add onions, butter, mushrooms, salt, and pepper. Cook for 3-5 minutes. Add lemon juice and scallops. Lock the lid and set it to Manual mode.

2. Cook for 15 minutes (high). Top with a drizzle of cream and fresh parsley.

Per serving: Calories: 312 kcal; Fat: 10 g; Carbs: 7 g; Protein: 31 g; Sugar: 1 g

87.   Pan-Seared Halibut with Citrus Butter Sauce

Preparation time: 10 minutes

Cooking time: 15 minutes

Servings: 3

Ingredients:

- 4 (5-ounce) halibut fillets, each 1-inch thick
- Sea salt
- Pepper
- ¼ cup butter
- 2 tsps. minced garlic
- 1 shallot, minced
- 1 tbsp freshly squeezed lemon juice
- 1 tbsp freshly squeezed orange juice
- 2 tsps. chopped fresh parsley
- 2 tbsps. olive oil

Directions:

1. Pat fish dry with paper towels and lightly season fillets with salt and pepper. Set aside on a paper towel-lined plate.

2. Place a small saucepan over medium heat and melt butter.

3. Sauté garlic and shallot until tender, 3 minutes.

4. Whisk in lemon juice and orange juice and bring sauce to a simmer, cooking until it thickens slightly, 2 minutes.

5. Remove sauce from Heat and Stir parsley; set aside.

6. Place a large skillet over medium-high heat and add olive oil.

7. Panfry fish until lightly browned and just cooked through, turning them over once, 10 minutes in total.

8. Serve fish immediately with a spoonful of sauce each.

Per serving: Calories: 319 kcal; Fat: 26 g; Carbs: 2 g; Protein: 22 g; Sugar: 1 g

88. Whitefish Curry

Preparation time: 10 minutes

Cooking time: 15 minutes

Servings: 6

Ingredients:

- 1 chopped onion
- 1 lb. Firm white fish fillets
- ¼ c. chopped fresh cilantro
- 1 c. vegetable broth
- 2 minced garlic cloves
- 1 tbsp. Minced fresh ginger
- 1 tsp. Salt
- ¼ tsp. pepper
- Lemon wedges
- 1 bruised lemongrass
- 2 c. cubed butternut squash
- 2 tsp. curry powder
- 2 tbsps. coconut oil
- 2 c. chopped broccoli
- 2oz. coconut milk
- 1 thinly sliced scallion

Directions:

1. In a pot, add coconut oil and melt.

2. Add curry powder, onion, garlic, ginger, and seasonings, and sauté 5 minutes

3. Add broccoli, butternut squash lemongrass and sauté two more minutes

4. Stir broth and coconut milk and bring to a boil. Lower heat to simmer and add fish.

5. Cover pot, simmer for 5 minutes, and discard lemongrass.

6. Spoon curry into a medium serving bowl.

7. Add scallion and cilantro to garnish the bee serving with lemon wedges.

8. Enjoy.

Per serving: Calories: 218 kcal; Fat: 9 g; Carbs: 18 g; Protein: 18 g; Sugar: 1 g

89. Easy Shrimp

Preparation time: 4 minutes

Cooking time: 5 minutes

Servings: 2

Ingredients:

- 1 lb. Shrimp, peeled and deveined
- 2 Garlic cloves, crushed
- 1 tbsp. Butter.
- A pinch of red Pepper
- Salt and Pepper, to taste
- 1 cup Parsley, chopped

Directions:

1. Melt butter and add shrimp, red pepper, garlic, salt, and pepper. Cook for 5 minutes, occasionally stirring shrimp until pink. Serve topped with parsley.

Per serving: Calories: 245 kcal; Fat: 4 g; Carbs: 5 g; Protein: 45 g; Sugar: 1 g

90. Marinated Fish Steaks

Preparation time: 10 minutes

Cooking time: 15 minutes

Servings: 4

Ingredients:

- 4 lime wedges
- 2 tbsps. Lime juice
- 2 minced garlic cloves
- 2 tsp. Olive oil
- 1 tbsp. snipped fresh oregano
- 1 lb. fresh swordfish
- 1 tsp. lemon-pepper seasoning

Directions:

1. Cut fish into four serving-size pieces, if necessary.

2. Put and combine lime juice, oregano, oil, lemon-pepper seasoning, and garlic in a shallow dish. Add fish; turn to coat with marinade.

3. Refrigerate for 30 minutes to 1-1/2 hours, turning steaks occasionally. Drain fish, reserving marinade.

4. Put fish on greased, unheated rack of a broiler pan.

5. Broil 4 inches from heat for 8 to 12 minutes or until fish flakes when tested, turning once and brushing with reserved marinade halfway through cooking.

6. Take off any remaining marinade.

7. Bee serving, squeeze lime juice on each steak.

Per serving: Calories: 240 kcal; Fat: 6 g; Carbs: 19 g; Protein: 12 g; Sugar: 4 g

91.   Delicious Creamy Crab Meat

Preparation time: 5 minutes

Cooking time: 10 minutes

Servings: 3

Ingredients:

- 1 lb. Crab meat
- ½ cup Cream cheese
- 2 tbsp. Mayonnaise
- Salt and Pepper, to taste
- 1 tbsp. Lemon juice
- 1 cup Cheddar cheese, shredded

Directions:

1. Mix cream cheese, mayo, lemon juice, salt and pepper. Add crab meat and make small balls. Place balls inside the pot. Seal the lid and press Manual.

2. Cook for 10 minutes (high). When done, allow pressure to release naturally for 10 minutes. Sprinkle cheese over and serve!

Per serving: Calories: 443 kcal; Fat: 30 g; Carbs: 3 g; Protein: 41 g; Sugar: 1 g

92.   Rosemary-Lemon Cod

Preparation time: 5 minutes

Cooking time: 10 minutes

Servings: 4

Ingredients:

- 2 tbsp. Extra Virgin Olive Oil
- 1½ pound Cod, Skin and Bone Removed, cut in 4 fillets

- 1 tbsp. Fresh Rosemary Leaves, chopped
- ½ tsp. Pepper, or more to taste
- ½ tsp. Sea Salt
- 1 Lemon Juice

Directions:

1. Heat olive oil in a huge nonstick skillet at medium-high heat until it shimmers.

2. Season cod with rosemary, pepper, and salt. Put fish in skillet and cook 3-5 minutes per side until opaque.

3. Pour lemon juice over cod fillets and cook for 1 minute.

Per serving: Calories: 24 kcal; Fat: 9 g; Carbs: 1 g; Protein: 39 g; Sugar: 1 g

93.   Cheesy Garlic Salmon

Preparation time: 15 minutes

Cooking time: 12 minutes

Servings: 4

Ingredients:

- ½ cup Asiago cheese
- 2 tbsps. freshly squeezed lemon juice
- 2 tbsps. butter at room temperature
- 2 tsps. minced garlic
- 1 tsp chopped fresh basil
- 1 tsp chopped fresh oregano
- 4 (5-ounce) salmon fillets
- 1 tbsp olive oil

Directions:

1. Preheat oven to 350°F.

2. In a small bowl, stir together Asiago cheese, lemon juice, butter, basil, and oregano.

3. Pat salmon dry and place fillets on baking sheet skin-side down. Divide the topping evenly between fillets and spread it across the fish using a knife or the back of a spoon.

4. Drizzle fish with olive oil and bake until the topping is golden and the fish is just cooked through 12 minutes.

5. Serve.

Per serving: Calories: 357 kcal; Fat: 28 g; Carbs: 2 g; Protein: 24 g; Sugar: 1 g

94.   Shrimp with Linguine

Preparation time: 10 minutes

Cooking time: 10 minutes

Servings: 4

Ingredients:

- 1 lb. Shrimp, cleaned
- 1 lb. Linguine
- 1 tbsp. Butter
- ½ cup Parmesan cheese, shredded
- 2 Garlic cloves, minced
- 1 cup Parsley, chopped
- Salt and Pepper, to taste
- ½ cup Coconut Cream, garnish
- ½ Avocado, diced, garnish
- 2 tbsp. fresh Dill, garnish

Directions:

1. Melt butter on Sauté. Stir linguine, garlic cloves, and parsley. Cook for 4 minutes until aromatic. Add shrimp; season with salt and pepper and seal the lid.

2. Select Manual and cook for 5 minutes (high). When ready, quickly release pressure. Unseal and remove the lid. Press Sauté, add cheese and stir well until combined, 30-40 seconds. Serve topped with coconut cream, avocado, and dill.

Per serving: Calories: 412 kcal; Fat: 21 g; Carbs: 6 g; Protein: 48 g; Sugar: 1 g

95.   Chili Shrimp and Pineapple

Preparation time: 10 minutes

Cooking time: 10 minutes

Servings: 4

Ingredients:

- 1-pound shrimp, peeled and deveined
- 2 tbsps. chili paste
- Pinch of sea salt
- Pinch of pepper
- 1 tbsp olive oil
- 1 cup pineapple, peeled and cubed
- ½ tsp ginger, grated
- 2 tsps. almonds, chopped
- 2 tbsps. cilantro, chopped

Directions:

1. Warm a pan with oil on medium-high heat; add ginger and chili paste, stir and cook for 2 minutes.

2. Add shrimp and/or ingredients, toss, cook, mix 8 minutes more, divide among bowls, and serve.

Per serving: Calories: 261 kcal; Fat: 4 g; Carbs: 15 g; Protein: 8 g; Sugar: 1 g

CHAPTER 6: Soups

96. Mediterranean Tomato Soup

Preparation time: 5 minutes

Cooking time: 30 minutes

Servings: 2

Ingredients:

- 2 red bell peppers, unseeded, chopped
- 2 medium onions, chopped
- 2-3 garlic cloves, minced
- 7-8 tomatoes, chopped
- 0.4 quarts chicken broth
- Salt and pepper, to taste
- 3 tbsps. olive oil
- 2 tbsp vinegar

Directions:

1. Heat oil, cook garlic, onion, and bell peppers 5-6 minutes or until bell peppers is roasted well.

2. Add tomatoes, salt, pepper, and vinegar; stir fry 4-5 minutes.

3. Add chicken broth and cover with lid. Let it cook 20 minutes on low heat.

4. When tomatoes are cooked well, puree soup with help of an electric beater.

5. Simmer 1-2 minutes.

6. Add to serving dish and top with desired herbs.

7. Serve and enjoy.

Per serving: Calories: 318 kcal; Fat: 97 g; Carbs: 60 g; Protein: 2 g; Sugar: 1 g

97. Quick Miso Soup with Wilted Greens

Preparation time: 10 minutes

Cooking time: 5 minutes

Servings: 4

Ingredients:

- 3 cups filtered water
- 3 cups vegetable broth
- 1 cup sliced mushrooms
- ½ tsp fish sauce
- 3 tbsps. miso paste
- 1 cup fresh baby spinach, thoroughly washed
- 4 scallions, sliced

Directions:

1. Heat pot, add water, broth, mushrooms, and fish sauce, and bring to boil. Remove from heat.

2. In small bowl, mix miso paste with ½ cup of heated broth mixture to dissolve miso. Stir miso mixture back in soup.

3. Stir spinach and scallions. Serve immediately.

Per serving: Calories: 44 kcal; Fat: 0 g; Carbs: 8 g; Protein: 2 g; Sugar: 1 g

98. Carrot and Ginger Soup

Preparation time: 10 minutes

Cooking time: 30 minutes

Servings: 6-8

Ingredients:

- 4½ cups plus 2 tbsps. water, divided
- 1 large onion, peeled and roughly chopped
- 8 carrots, peeled and roughly chopped
- 1½-inch piece fresh ginger, sliced thin
- 1¼ tsps. sea salt
- 2 cups unsweetened coconut milk

Directions:

1. Add 2 tbsps. of water to large pot, add onion and sauté over medium heat 4 minutes or until translucent.

2. Add carrots, ginger, salt, and remaining water to pot. Bring to boil, reduce heat to low. Cover and simmer 20 minutes.

3. When simmering is over, open lid, mix in coconut milk and cook 4 more minutes.

4. Pour soup in blender, pulse to purée until creamy and smooth. Serve soup in large bowl immediately.

Per serving: Calories: 228 kcal; Fat: 19 g; Carbs: 15 g; Protein: 3 g; Sugar: 1 g

99. Root Vegetable Soup

Preparation time: 15 minutes

Cooking time: 15 minutes

Servings:

Ingredients:

- 1 tbsp avocado oil
- 1 medium yellow onion, chopped
- 2 garlic cloves, minced
- 1 (1-inch) piece fresh ginger,
- 2 lbs. carrots, coarsely chopped
- 2 medium red potatoes, chopped
- 2 medium yellow beets, peeled and chopped
- 1 large parsnip, peeled and chopped
- 4 cups vegetable broth
- 1 cup water
- 1 tsp sea salt
- ¼ tsp ground turmeric
- ¼ tsp pepper
- ½ cup coconut milk

Directions:

1. Select Sauté on Instant Pot, pour in oil, and let pot preheat.

2. Add onion, garlic, and ginger and cook 4 minutes.

3. Add carrots, potatoes, beets, parsnip, broth, water, salt, turmeric, and pepper. Select Cancel. Lock lid.

4. Select Pressure Cook, cook at high 15 minutes.

5. When cooking is complete, use a quick release.

6. Remove lid and Stir coconut milk. Serve immediately.

Per serving: Calories: 350 kcal; Fat: 10 g; Carbs: 61 g; Protein: 6 g; Sugar: 1 g

100. Super Green Soup

Preparation time: 15 minutes

Cooking time: 30 minutes

Servings: 6

Ingredients:

- 2 cups unsweetened coconut milk
- 3 cups water
- 1½ tsps. sea salt, or to taste
- 1 bunch fresh parsley, rinsed, stemmed and roughly chopped
- 4 cups tightly packed kale,
- 4 cups tightly packed spinach, rinsed, stemmed and roughly chopped
- 4 cups tightly packed collard greens, rinsed, stemmed and roughly chopped

Directions:

1. Pour coconut milk and water in large pot, sprinkle with salt. Bring to boil over high heat. Reduce heat to low.

2. Add 1 cup of each greens to pot and cook 5 minutes or until wilted. Repeat with remaining greens.

3. When all greens are wilted, simmer 10 minutes.

4. Pour soup in blender, pulse until creamy and smooth.

5. Pour soup in large bowl and serve immediately.

Per serving: Calories: 334 kcal; Fat: 29 g; Carbs: 18 g; Protein: 7 g; Sugar: 1 g

101. Dill Celery Soup

Preparation time: 10 minutes

Cooking time: 30 minutes

Servings: 4

Ingredients:

- 6 c. celery stalk, chopped
- 2 c. filtered alkaline water
- 1 medium onion, chopped
- 1/2 tsp. dill
- 1 c of coconut milk
- 1/4 tsp. sea salt

Directions:

1. Combine all elements into the instant pot and mix fine.

2. Cover the pot with a lid and select the soup mode that takes 30 minutes.

3. Release pressure using the quick release setting then open the lid carefully.

4. Blend the soup utilizing a submersion blender until smooth.

5. Stir well and serve.

Per serving: Calories: 193 kcal; Fat: 15 g; Carbs: 11 g; Protein: 5 g; Sugar: 6 g

102. Roasted Vegetable Soup

Preparation time: 15 minutes

Cooking time: 20 minutes

Servings: 2

Ingredients:

- tbsp olive oil
- 5 garlic cloves, peeled
- 0.3 lb. Potatoes diced (1 cm thick)
- yellow bell peppers, diced
- ½ tsps. fresh rosemary, finely chopped
- carrot, halved lengthwise and cut in 1 cm piece
- 1 red onion, in chunks
- 0.4 quarts carrot juice
- 0.3 lb. Italian tomatoes, diced
- 1 tsp fresh tarragon
- Salt and pepper, to taste

Directions:

1. Preheat oven 400° F.

2. In baking tray place potatoes, peppers, garlic, carrot, onion, and tomatoes. Drizzle with olive oil and roast 10-15 minutes.

3. In saucepan add carrot juice, tarragon; let boil a little.

4. Add all roasted vegetables and stir well. Let it simmer a few minutes.

5. Season with salt, pepper, and rosemary. Mix well.

6. Serve and enjoy.

Per serving: Calories: 318 kcal; Fat: 97 g; Carbs: 60 g; Protein: 2 g; Sugar: 2 g

103. Butternut Squash, Carrot, and Celery Soup

Preparation time: 20 minutes

Cooking time: 30 minutes

Servings: 6

Ingredients:

- 4½ cups plus 2 tbsps. water, divided
- 1 onion, roughly chopped
- 1 large butternut squash, washed, peeled, ends trimmed, halved, seeded, and cut in ½-inch chunks
- 3 carrots, peeled and roughly chopped
- 2 celery stalks, roughly chopped
- 1 tsp sea salt, or to taste

Directions:

1. Add 2 tbsps. of water to large pot, add onion and sauté over medium heat 5 minutes or until tender.

2. Add butternut squash, carrots, celery, salt, and remaining water. Bring to boil. Reduce heat to low, simmer 25 minutes or until squash is soft.

3. Pour soup in food processor, pulse to purée until creamy and smooth.

4. Pour soup in large bowl and serve immediately.

Per serving: Calories: 104 kcal; Fat: 0 g; Carbs: 27 g; Protein: 2 g; Sugar: 1 g

104. Tomato and Cabbage Puree Soup

Preparation time: 5 minutes

Cooking time: 30 minutes

Servings: 2

Ingredients:

- 0.6 lb. Tomatoes, chopped
- 3-4 garlic cloves, minced
- 0.2 lb. Cabbage, chopped
- 4 tbsps. olive oil
- red onion, chopped
- Salt and pepper, to taste
- Spice mix of choice
- 4 quarts of vegetable broth

Directions:

1. Heat oil, cook garlic, onion, and cabbage 4-5 minutes. Make sure that cabbage is nicely softened.

2. Add tomatoes and stir fry until liquid is reduced and tomatoes are dissolved.

3. Add salt, pepper, spice mix, and vegetable broth.

4. Cover saucepan with lid and let mixture cook on low flame 30 minutes.

5. Puree soup with help of an electric beater.

6. Serve and enjoy.

Per serving: Calories: 218 kcal; Fat: 15 g; Carbs: 220 g; Protein: 2 g; Sugar: 1 g

105. Anian Avgolemono Sour Soup

Preparation time: 20 minutes

Cooking time: 50 minutes

Servings: 2

Ingredients:

- 8-cups water
- 1-pc whole chicken, cut in pieces
- Salt and pepper
- 1-cup whole grain rice
- 4-pcs eggs, separated
- 2-pcs lemons, juice
- ¼-cup fresh dill, minced
- Dill sprigs and lemon slices garnish

Directions:

1. Pour water in large pot. Add chicken pieces, and cover pot. Simmer an hour

2. Remove cooked chicken pieces from pot and take 2-cups of chicken broth. Set aside and let it cool

3. Bring to boil remaining. Add salt and pepper to taste. Add rice and cover pot. Simmer 20 minutes

4. Meanwhile, de-bone cooked chicken and tear flesh in small pieces. Set aside.

5. Work on separated egg whites and yolks whisk egg whites until stiff; whisk yolks with lemon juice.

6. Pour egg yolk mixture to egg white mixture. Whisk well until fully combined.

7. Add reserved 2-cups of chicken broth to mixture, whisking constantly to prevent eggs from curdling.

8. After fully incorporating egg mixture and chicken broth, pour this mixture in simmering broth and rice. Add dill, and stir well. Simmer without bringing it to boil.

9. Add chicken pieces to soup. Mix until fully combined.

10. To serve, ladle soup in bowls and sprinkle with fresh pepper. Garnish with lemon slices and dill sprigs.

Per serving: Calories: 122 kcal; Fat: 2 g; Carbs: 8 g; Protein: 13 g; Sugar: 1 g

106. Potato and Broccoli Soup

Preparation time: 10 minutes

Cooking time: 10 minutes

Servings:

Ingredients:

- 2 tbsps. avocado oil
- 1 small yellow onion, diced
- 2 garlic cloves, minced
- 4 lbs Yukon Gold potatoes, diced
- 1 large head broccoli, cut in florets
- 4 cups vegetable broth
- 1 tbsp raw apple cider vinegar
- 1 tsp sea salt
- Pepper

Directions:

1. Select Sauté on Instant Pot and let pot preheat.

2. Pour in oil and add onion and garlic. Cook 4 minutes.

3. Add potatoes, broccoli, broth, vinegar, salt, and pepper to pot. Select Cancel. Lock lid.

4. Select Pressure Cook, cook at high 8 minutes.

5. When cooking is complete, use a quick release.

6. Remove lid and serve warm.

Per serving: Calories: 422 kcal; Fat: 7 g; Carbs: 88 g; Protein: 9 g; Sugar: 1 g

107. Garlic Soup

Preparation time: 15 minutes

Cooking time: 0 minutes

Servings: 2

Ingredients:

- 5 cups water
- Head garlic, unpeeled
- Sprigs fresh thyme
- 2 Tbsps. fur virgin olive oil
- Salt
- Pepper
- 2 egg yolks
- Slices of bread, gently toasted

Directions:

1. Bring water to boil with garlic and thyme and simmer twenty minutes.

2. Take away garlic and peel. Place flesh in an exceedingly bowl and mash.

3. Step by step add vegetable oil and blend well. Return to soup.

4. Take away thyme and then you should Season it with salt & pepper.

5. Beat egg yolks in bowl and step by step add a ladleful of soup.

6. Combine well and Stir soup. Simmer some minutes, however don't let it boil or soup can curdle.

7. Place slices of toasts in individual bowls and pour over soup. Serve at once.

Per serving: Calories: 123 kcal; Fat: 3 g; Carbs: 19 g; Protein: 5 g; Sugar: 1 g

108. Red Soup, Seville Style

Preparation time: 15 minutes

Cooking time: 15 minutes

Servings: 2

Ingredients:

- 2 ounces stale bread, crusts removed
- 3 tbsps. virgin olive oil
- 3 tbsps. wine vinegar
- 2 garlic cloves, crushed
- 2 tsp salt
- Tsp cayenne pepper pinch of cumin
- Little red onion, chopped
- Pound ripe tomatoes, peeled, seeded, and chopped
- Cucumber, peeled, seeded, and chopped
- Red peppers, cored, seeded, and chopped
- Cups ice water
- garnish
- 4 tbsps. red peppers, cored, seeded, and finely chopped
- 4 tbsps. finely cut cucumber
- 4 tbsps. finely cut purple onion
- 2 tbsps. finely cut contemporary mint leaves

Directions:

1. First, you should Soak bread in water and then squeeze dry.

2. Place in blender or kitchen appliance

3. With vegetable oil, vinegar, garlic, salt, and spices and method to sleek cream.

4. Add onion, tomatoes, cucumber, peppers, 1/2 drinking water, and still method vegetables till sleek.

5. Pour in a soup serving dish and add remaining water.

6. Chill bee serving. Place garnishes in little dishes and serve with soup.

Per serving: Calories: 123 kcal; Fat: 3 g; Carbs: 19 g; Protein: 5 g; Sugar: 1 g

109. Spicy Carrot Soup

Preparation time: 10 minutes

Cooking time: 20 minutes

Servings: 6

Ingredients:

- 8 large carrots, peeled and chopped
- 1 1/2 c. filtered alkaline water
- 14 oz. coconut milk
- 3 garlic cloves, peeled
- 1 tbsp. red curry paste

- 1/4 c. olive oil
- 1 onion, chopped
- Salt

Directions:

1. Combine all the ingredients into the instant pot and mix well.

2. Cover the pot with a lid, select manual, and set the timer for 15 minutes.

3. Allow releasing pressure naturally then open the lid.

4. Blend the soup utilizing a submersion blender until smooth.

5. Serve and enjoy.

Per serving: Calories: 267 kcal; Fat: 22 g; Carbs: 13 g; Protein: 4 g; Sugar: 5 g

110. Brown Miso Soup with Mushrooms

Preparation time: 15 minutes

Cooking time: 28 minutes

Servings: 6

Ingredients:

- 1 tbsp avocado oil
- 1 yellow onion, chopped
- 1 carrot, diced
- 3 garlic cloves, minced
- 8 ounces cremini mushrooms, sliced
- 8 ounces shiitake mushrooms, sliced
- 1 tsp dried thyme
- ½ tsp sea salt
- 1tsp pepper
- 4 cups vegetable broth
- 3 cups water
- ½ cup barley or brown rice
- 1 tbsp brown rice miso paste

Directions:

1. Select Sauté on Instant Pot, pour in oil, and let pot preheat.

2. Add onion and carrot and cook 4 minutes. Add garlic and cook 1 minute. Add cremini and shiitake mushrooms, thyme, salt, and pepper and cook 4 minutes, stirring occasionally.

3. Stir broth, water, barley, and miso. Select Cancel. Lock lid.

4. Select Pressure Cook, cook at high 18 minutes.

5. When cooking is complete, use a natural release 10 minutes, quick release any remaining pressure.

6. Remove lid and serve hot.

Per serving: Calories: 129 kcal; Fat: 3 g; Carbs: 23 g; Protein: 4 g; Sugar: 1 g

CHAPTER 7: Snacks

111. Brie with Apricot Topping

Preparation time: 25 minutes

Cooking time: 0 cooking

Servings: 2-3

Ingredients:

- 1/2 cup of chopped dried apricots
- 2 tbsp. water
- 1 tsp. balsamic vinegar
- Dash salt
- 1/2 to 1 tsp. minced fresh rosemary or 1/4 tsp. dried rosemary, crushed
- 1 round Brie cheese (8 ounces)
- Assorted crackers

Directions:

1. Heat oven to 400F. Mix all first five ingredients in a small saucepan; bring it to a boil. Cook and when slightly thickened, stir with medium heat. Remove from heat; add rosemary and stir.

2. From the top of the cheese, cut the rind off. Put cheese in an ovenproof, non-greased serving dish. Spoon apricot mix with cheese. Bake until cheese is softened, 10-12 minutes, uncovered. Serve soft, crackers included.

Per serving: Calories: 529 kcal; Fat: 8 g; Carbs: 9 g; Protein: 1 g; Sugar: 6 g

112. Tomato and Mozzarella Bites

Preparation time: 30 minutes

Cooking time: 15 minutes

Servings: 2-3

Ingredients:

- 20 grape tomatoes, halved
- fresh basil leaves (20)
- 20 small balls of fresh mozzarella cheese
- salt and pepper as needed
- balsamic vinegar (½ cup)
- ¼ cup of extra virgin olive oil
- 20 toothpicks

Directions:

1. Use a toothpick to spear half a tomato, a basil leaf, a ball of mozzarella, and half a tomato. With ingredients, repeat.

2. Place and sprinkle with salt and pepper on a serving plate. In a small bowl, mix vinegar and oil into a dipping sauce.

Per serving: Calories: 225 kcal; Fat: 18 g; Carbs: 5 g; Protein: 47 g; Sugar: 0 g

113. Pickle Roll-Ups

Preparation time: 20 minutes

Cooking time: 0 minutes

Servings: 2-3

Ingredients:

- ¼ pound deli ham (nitrate-free), thinly sliced (8 slices)
- 8 ounces Neufchâtel cheese at room temperature
- 1 tsp dried dill
- 1 tsp onion powder
- 8 whole kosher dill pickle spears

Directions:

1. Get a large cutting board or clean counter space to assemble roll-ups.

2. Lay ham slices on a work surface and carefully spread them on Neufchâtel cheese.

3. Season each lightly with dill and onion powder.

4. Place an entire pickle on the end of the ham and carefully roll.

5. Slice each pickle roll-up into mini rounds ½- to 1-inch wide.

6. Skew each with a toothpick for easier serving.

Per serving: Calories: 86 kcal; Fat: 7 g; Carbs: 4 g; Protein: 4 g; Sugar: 2 g

114. Lentil and Eggplant Stew

Preparation time: 15 minutes

Cooking time: 35 minutes

Servings: 2

Ingredients:

- 1 lb. eggplant
- 1 lb. dry lentils
- 1 c. chopped vegetables
- 1 c. low sodium vegetable broth

Directions:

1. Incorporate all the ingredients in your instant pot, and cook on Stew for 35 minutes.
2. Release the pressure naturally and serve.

Per serving: Calories: 310 kcal; Fat: 10 g; Carbs: 22 g; Protcin: 14 g; Sugar: 2 g

115. Spinach and Artichoke Dip

Preparation time: 10 minutes

Cooking time: 5 minutes

Servings: 2-3

Ingredients:

- 10 ounces – Baby spinach
- 14 ounces – Artichokes, frozen
- 8 ounces – Light cream cheese
- ½ cup – Onion, finely chopped
- ½ cup – Parmesan cheese
- 1 tbsp – Lemon juice
- 3 cloves – Garlic, finely grated
- ½ tsp – Red pepper flakes
- ½ tsp – Oregano
- ½ tsp – Ground pepper
- ¼ tsp – Salt

Directions:

1. Wash, dry, and steam baby spinach.
2. In a medium-sized nonstick saucepan, pour cooking oil, and sauté onion and garlic for 5 minutes on low-medium heat for 5 minutes.
3. In a food processor, put spinach and chop.
4. Now add artichokes and blend them for a few moments.

5. Transfer blended artichokes and spinach to a medium-sized bowl.

6. Add oregano, lemon juice, red pepper, and cream cheese and stir well.

7. Cook it at low-medium temperature until it starts bubbling.

8. Now add salt, parmesan cheese, and pepper.

9. Serve fresh

Per serving: Calories: 122 kcal; Fat: 4 g; Carbs: 18 g; Protein: 12 g; Sugar: 1 g

116. Marinated Mushrooms

Preparation time: 10 minutes

Cooking time: 15 minutes

Servings: 2-3

Ingredients:

- 1 cup - Beef soup
- 1 tsp - Parsley flakes
- 1 pound - Mushrooms
- 1 tsp – Onion powder
- 8 ounces – Water
- 1 tsp – Garlic powder
- ¼ tsp – Salt

Directions:

1. In a medium bowl, dissolve beef soup in water
2. Put all remaining ingredients in soup and water mix. Cover it and boil in low-medium heat for 2 hours.

Per serving: Calories: 186 kcal; Fat: 2 g; Carbs: 31 g; Protein: 8 g; Sugar: 1 g

117. No Dish Summer Medley

Preparation time: 10 minutes

Cooking time: 10 minutes

Servings: 2-3

Ingredients:

- 2 cups - Chicken soup
- ½ cup – Sliced celery
- ½ cup - Yellow summer squash
- ½ cup – Mushrooms, chopped
- ¼ tsp – Salt

- ¼ tsp – Pepper powder

Directions:

1. In a medium saucepan, mix all ingredients except chicken soup.

2. Now pour chicken soup over it.

3. Add salt and pepper.

4. Cover and cook for 20 minutes until it starts to boil

Per serving: Calories: 212 kcal; Fat: 4 g; Carbs: 18 g; Protein: 8 g; Sugar: 1 g

118. Curry Roasted Cauliflower Florets

Preparation time: 5 minutes

Cooking time: 25 minutes

Servings: 6

Ingredients:

- 8 c. cauliflower florets
- 2 tbsps. olive oil
- 1 tsp. curry powder
- 1/2 teaspoon garlic powder
- Salt and pepper

Directions:

1. Prep the oven to 425 °F and line a baking sheet with foil.

2. Toss the cauliflower with olive oil and spread on the baking sheet.

3. Sprinkle with curry powder, garlic powder, salt, and pepper.

4. Roast for 25 minutes or until just tender. Serve hot.

Per serving: Calories: 75 kcal; Fat: 9 g; Carbs: 8 g; Protein: 16 g; Sugar: 7 g

119. Mashed Cauliflower

Preparation time: 10 minutes

Cooking time: 5 minutes

Servings: 2-3

Ingredients:

- 1 large head cauliflower
- ¼ cup water

- 1/3 cup low-fat buttermilk
- 1 tbsp minced garlic
- 1 tbsp extra-virgin olive oil

Directions:

1. Break cauliflower in small florets. Place in large microwave-safe bowl with water. Cover and microwave 5 minutes, or until cauliflower is soft. Drain water from bowl.

2. In blender or food processor, puree buttermilk, cauliflower, garlic, and olive oil on medium speed until cauliflower is smooth and creamy.

3. Serve immediately.

Per serving: Calories: 65 kcal; Fat: 2 g; Carbs: 8 g; Protein: 3 g; Sugar: 3 g

120. Homemade Potato Chips

Preparation time: 30 minutes

Cooking time: 5 min/ batch

Servings: 2-3

Ingredients:

- 7 unpeeled medium potatoes (2 lbs)
- ice water (2 quarts)
- Salt (5 tsp.)
- Garlic powder (2 tsp.)
- 1-1/2 tsp. celery salt
- 1-1/2 tsp. pepper
- Oil deep-fat frying

Directions:

1. Slice potatoes in thin slices, using a vegetable peeler or a metal cheese slicer. Place it in wide bowl; add salt and ice water. 30 minutes, soak.

2. Place potatoes on paper towels and pat them dry. Combine garlic powder, celery salt and pepper in small bowl; set aside.

3. Heat 1-1/2 in. in cast-iron. Up to 375 ° crude. Fry potatoes until golden brown in clusters, stirring constantly 3-4 minutes.

4. With slotted spoon, remove; drain onto paper towels. Sprinkle with seasoning mixture immediately. Store it in air-tight jar.

Per serving: Calories: 176 kcal; Fat: 8 g; Carbs: 3 g; Protein: 42 g; Sugar: 1 g

121. Everything Parmesan Crisps

Preparation time: 10 minutes

Cooking time: 5 minutes

Servings: 2-3

Ingredients:

- 1 tsp poppy seeds
- 1 tsp sesame seeds
- 1 tsp garlic flakes
- 1 tsp onion flakes
- 12 tbsps. grated Parmesan cheese

Directions:

1. Preheat oven 400°F.

2. Mix poppy seeds, sesame seeds, garlic flakes, and onion flakes in a small bowl.

3. Line sheet pan with silicon baking mat or parchment paper. Pour 1 tbsp of Parmesan onto mat, and gently pat down with fingers to make a 2- to 2½-inch round.

4. Repeat making sure to keep 1 inch between each round.

5. Bake 3 minutes. Remove from oven, and sprinkle ¼ tsp of seasoning over each Parmesan round.

6. Bake 3-5 minutes, or until golden and crisp, and serve.

Per serving: Calories: 23 kcal; Fat: 2 g; Carbs: 0 g; Protein: 2 g; Sugar: 0 g

122. Low Cholesterol Scalloped Potatoes

Preparation time: 10 minutes

Cooking time: 35 minutes

Servings: 2-3

Ingredients:

- 4 cups - Potatoes
- ½ cup – Onion, coarsely chopped
- 1 tbsp – Parsley chopped
- 1½ cup – Skim milk
- 3 tbsps. – Low cholesterol margarine
- ¼ tsp – Pepper
- ½ tsp – Salt
- 3 tbsps. – Whole grain flour

Directions:

1. Wash, clean potatoes and finely slice potatoes.

2. Stack potatoes and onion layer by layer in casserole.

3. Drizzle flour between onion and potatoes.

4. Pour milk in medium bowl and add parsley, pepper, and salt and bring to low-medium heat. Once milk becomes hot, pour it over potato-onion layer.

5. Cover casserole and bake it one hour at 350°F. Remove cover and bake it 3 minutes.

Per serving: Calories: 184 kcal; Fat: 6 g; Carbs: 32 g; Protein: 6 g; Sugar: 1 g

123. Steamed Asparagus

Preparation time: 3 minutes

Cooking time: 2 minutes

Servings: 4

Ingredients:

- 1 lb. fresh asparagus, rinsed and tough ends trimmed
- 1 c. water

Directions:

1. Place the asparagus into a wire steamer rack and set it inside your instant pot.

2. Add water to the pot. Close and seal the lid, turning the steam release valve to the "Sealing" position.

3. Select the Steam function to cook on high pressure for 2 minutes.

4. Once done, do a quick pressure release of the steam.

5. Lift the wire steamer basket out of the pot and place the asparagus onto a serving plate.

6. Season as desired and serve.

Per serving: Calories: 22 kcal; Fat: 20 g; Carbs: 4 g; Protein: 2 g; Sugar: 13 g

124. Moch Mashed Potatoes

Preparation time: 5 minutes

Cooking time: 18 minutes

Servings: 2-3

Ingredients:

- 1 cup - Tomato chicken soup
- 4 ounces – Frozen cauliflower
- ¼ tsp - Salt
- 6 cup – Water

Directions:

1. Cook cauliflower 15 minutes in small saucepan by adding salt until it becomes soft.
2. Drain excess water after cooking.
3. Mash cooked cauliflower. Add chicken soup in masked cauliflower and heat mix 2 minutes. Serve hot.

Per serving: Calories: 165 kcal; Fat: 3 g; Carbs: 33 g; Protein: 12 g; Sugar: 1 g

125. Lower Carb Hummus

Preparation time: 9 minutes

Cooking time: 60 minutes

Servings: 2

Ingredients:

- 0.5 c. dry chickpeas
- 1 c. vegetable stock
- 1 c. pumpkin puree
- 2 tbsp. smoked paprika
- Salt and pepper to taste

Directions:

1. Soak the chickpeas overnight.
2. Place the chickpeas and stock in the instant pot.
3. Cook on Beans for 60 minutes.
4. Depressurize naturally.
5. Blend the chickpeas with the remaining ingredients.

Per serving: Calories: 135 kcal; Fat: 3 g; Carbs: 18 g; Protein: 12 g; Sugar: 2 g

126. Cheese Chips

Preparation time: 20 min

Cooking time: 30 min

Servings: 2-3

Ingredients:

- 10 tbsp parmesan cheese shredded
- Garlic powder
- 2 tbsp fresh basil finely chopped

Directions:

1. Heat oven 350 degrees. Line baking sheet with parchment paper.
2. Scoop one tbsp of cheese and drop in plop on baking sheet.
3. With fingers, gently spread cheese in a thin circle and add a pinch of garlic powder and a pinch of basil.
4. Repeat until all of cheese is gone.
5. Place sheet in oven until circle edges are golden brown. Give them a minute to cool.

Per serving: Calories: 212 kcal; Fat: 2 g; Carbs: 23 g; Protein: 26 g; Sugar: 1 g

127. Maple-Mashed Sweet Potatoes

Preparation time: 5 minutes

Cooking time: 5 minutes

Servings: 2-3

Ingredients:

- 1 pound – Sweet potatoes
- 1 cup – Carrots, thinly sliced
- 2 tbsps. – Maple syrup
- ¼ tsp – Nutmeg
- ¼ tsp – Fresh pepper
- 4 cup – Water

Directions:

1. Wash and clean sweet potatoes.
2. Peel and cut in small chunks.
3. In large bowl, pour water and bring to boil.
4. Put carrots and sweet potatoes in it.
5. Reduce Heat and continue cooking 10 minutes until carrots and sweet potatoes become soft.

6. Drain vegetables using a colander and put in a bowl.

7. Mas vegetables until it becomes smooth.

8. Sprinkle pepper and nutmeg in it and stir.

9. Drizzle maple syrup over it, and stir.

Per serving: Calories: 212 kcal; Fat: 4 g; Carbs: 18 g; Protein: 6 g; Sugar: 1 g

128. Baked Zucchini Fries

Preparation time: 15 minutes

Cooking time: 15 minutes

Servings: 2-3

Ingredients:

- 3 large zucchinis
- 2 large eggs
- 1 cup whole-wheat bread crumbs
- ¼ cup shredded Parmigiano-Reggiano cheese
- 1 tsp garlic powder
- 1 tsp onion powder

Directions:

1. Preheat oven 425°F. Line baking sheet with aluminum foil.

2. Halve each zucchini lengthwise and continue slicing each piece in fries ½ inch in diameter. You will have 8 strips per zucchini.

3. In small bowl, crack eggs and beat lightly.

4. In medium bowl, combine bread crumbs, Parmigiano-Reggiano cheese, garlic powder, and onion powder.

5. One by one, dip each zucchini strip in egg, roll it in bread crumb mixture. Place on prepared baking sheet.

6. Roast 30 minutes, stirring fries halfway through. Zucchini fries are done when brown and crispy.

7. Serve immediately.

Per serving: Calories: 89 kcal; Fat: 3 g; Carbs: 10 g; Protein: 5 g; Sugar: 3 g

129. Lentil and Chickpea Curry

Preparation time: 15 minutes

Cooking time: 20 minutes

Servings: 2

Ingredients:

- 2 c. dry lentils and chickpeas
- 1 thinly sliced onion
- 1 c. chopped tomato
- 3 tbsps. curry paste
- 1 tbsp. oil or ghee

Directions:

1. Press the instant pot to sauté and mix onion, oil, and curry paste.

2. Once the onion is cooked, stir the remaining ingredients and seal.

3. Cook on Stew for 20 minutes.

4. Release the pressure naturally and serve.

Per serving: Calories: 360 kcal; Fat: 19 g; Carbs: 26 g; Protein: 10 g; Sugar: 3 g

130. Chocolate Peanut Butter Protein Balls

Preparation time: 10 minutes

Cooking time: 5 minutes

Servings: 2-3

Ingredients:

- 1 1/2 cup of old-fashioned rolled oats
- 1 cup of natural peanut butter
- 1/4 cup of honey
- 2 scoops (64 g) chocolate Protein powder
- 2 Tbsp. chocolate chips

Directions:

1. Place oats, peanut butter, honey, chocolate chips and Protein powder in large bowl and stir to blend.

2. It takes a little arm muscle to get mixture to blend and it can seem too thick at first but as you keep mixing, it will come together. I used my hands at end to knead dough, which seemed to help.

3. Use a cookie scoop to scoop then shape dough in balls until mixed.

4. Store in freezer.

Per serving: Calories: 114 kcal; Fat: 6 g; Carbs: 8 g; Protein: 6 g; Sugar: 5 g

Desserts

131. Chocolate Cream

Preparation time: 1 Hour And 10 minutes

Cooking time: 2 hours

Servings: 2

Ingredients:

- 2 cups low-fat milk
- 3 ounces dark and unsweetened chocolate
- 1 cup warm water
- 3 tablespoons stevia
- 2 tablespoons gelatin
- 1 tablespoon vanilla extract

Directions:

1. Mix warm water with gelatin, stir well and leave aside for 1 hour.

2. Put this in your slow cooker, add milk, stevia, chocolate and vanilla, stir well, cover, cook on High for 2 hours, whisk cream one more time, divide into bowls and serve.

Per serving: Calories: 181 kcal; Fat: 13 g; Carbs: 19 g; Protein: 10 g; Sugar: 7 g

132. Shortbread Cookies

Preparation time: 10 minutes

Cooking time: 70 minutes

Servings: 6

Ingredients:

- 2 1/2 c. almond flour
- 6 tbsps. nut butter
- 1/2 c. erythritol
- 1 tsp. vanilla essence

Directions:

1. Preheat your oven to 350 °F.
2. Layer a cookie sheet with parchment paper.
3. Beat butter with erythritol until fluffy.
4. Stir in the vanilla essence and almond flour. Mix well until becomes crumbly.
5. Spoon out a tablespoon of cookie dough onto the cookie sheet.
6. Add more dough to make as many cookies.

7. Bake for 15 minutes until brown.
8. Serve.

Per serving: Calories: 288 kcal; Fat: 25 g; Carbs: 9 g; Protein: 7 g; Sugar: 1 g

133. Chocolate Chip Quinoa Granola Bars

Preparation time: 5 minutes

Cooking time: 10 minutes

Servings: 16

Ingredients:

- ½ cup of chia seeds
- ½ cup walnuts, chopped
- 1 cup buckwheat
- 1 cup uncooked quinoa
- 2/3 cup dairy-free margarine
- ½ cup flax seed
- 1 tsp of cinnamon
- ½ cup of honey
- ½ cup of chocolate chips
- 1 tsp of vanilla
- ¼ tsp salt

Directions:

1. Preheat oven 350 degrees F.
2. Spread walnuts, quinoa, wheat, flax, and chia on baking sheet.
3. Bake 10 minutes.
4. Line baking dish with plastic wrap. Apply cooking spray. Keep aside.
5. Melt margarine and honey in saucepot.
6. Whisk together vanilla, salt, and cinnamon in margarine mix.
7. Keep wheat mix and quinoa in bowl. Pour margarine sauce in it.
8. Stir mixture. Coat well. Cool Stir chocolate chips.
9. Spread mixture in baking dish. Press firmly in pan.
10. Plastic wrap. Refrigerator overnight.
11. Slice in bars and serve.

Per serving: Calories: 408 kcal; Fat: 18 g; Carbs: 32 g; Protein: 9 g; Sugar: 13 g

134. Gala Apple Flavored Ice Cubes

Preparation time: 4 hours 10 minutes

Cooking time: 0 minutes

Servings: 24

Ingredients:

- Apple (2, Gala)
- Honey (Four teaspoons.)
- Water (3 cups)

Directions:

1. Blend all ingredients.
2. Set a fine-mesh strainer in a bowl. Before transferring your juice into filter.
3. Gently press pulp to extract all possible liquid, then discard pulp.
4. Fill your empty ice trays with your juice.
5. Set to freeze for at least 3 hours until frozen.
6. Keep them in freezer until ready to serve.

Per serving: Calories: 83 kcal; Fat: 21 g; Carbs: 2 g; Protein: 1 g; Sugar: 2 g

135. Carrot Cake

Preparation time: 10 minutes

Cooking time: 2 hours and 30 minutes

Servings: 2

Ingredients:

- 1 cup pineapple, dried and chopped
- 4 carrots, chopped
- 1 cup dates, pitted and chopped
- ½ cup coconut flakes
- Cooking spray
- 1 and ½ cups whole wheat flour
- ½ teaspoon cinnamon powder

Directions:

1. Add carrots in your food processor and pulse.
2. Add dates, coconut, pineapple, flour, cinnamon and pulse very well again.

3. Grease slow cooker with cooking spray, put cake mix, spread, cover and cook on High for 2 hours and 30 minutes.

4. Set aside cake to cool down, slice and serve.

Per serving: Calories: 252 kcal; Fat: 3 g; Carbs: 55 g; Protein: 5 g; Sugar: 24 g

136. Homemade Protein Bar

Preparation time: 5 minutes

Cooking time: 10 minutes

Servings: 4

Ingredients:

- 1 c. nut butter
- 4 tbsps. coconut oil
- 2 scoops vanilla protein
- Stevia, to taste
- 1/2 teaspoon sea salt
- 1 tsp. cinnamon

Directions:

1. Mix coconut oil with butter, protein, stevia, and salt in a dish.
2. Stir in cinnamon and chocolate chip.
3. Press the mixture firmly and freeze until firm.
4. Cut the crust into small bars.
5. Serve and enjoy.

Per serving: Calories: 179 kcal; Fat: 16 g; Carbs: 5 g; Protein: 6 g; Sugar: 4 g

137. Lemon Vegan Cake

Preparation time: 10 minutes

Cooking time: 10 minutes

Servings: 3

Ingredients:

- 1 cup of pitted dates
- 2-1/2 cups pecans
- 1-1/2 cup agave
- 3 avocados, halved & pitted
- 3 cups of cauliflower rice, prepared
- 1 lemon juice and zest
- ½ lemon extract
- 1-1/2 cups pineapple, crushed

- 1-1/2 tsp vanilla extract
- Pinch of cinnamon
- 1-1/2 cups of dairy-free yogurt

Directions:

1. Line the baking sheet with parchment paper.

2. Pulse pecans in a food processor.

3. Add agave and dates. Pulse a minute.

4. Transfer this mix to a baking sheet. Wipe the bowl of the processor.

5. Bring together pineapple, agave, avocados, cauliflower, lemon juice, and zest in a food processor. Get a smooth mixture.

6. Now add lemon extract, cinnamon, and vanilla extract. Pulse.

7. Pour this mix into the pan on the crust.

8. Refrigerate for 5 hours minimum.

9. Take out the cake and keep it at room temperature for 20 minutes.

10. Take out the cake's outer ring.

11. Whisk together vanilla extract, agave, and yogurt in a bowl.

12. Pour on the cake.

Per serving: Calories: 688 kcal; Fat: 28 g; Carbs: 100 g; Protein: 28 g; Sugar: 40 g

138. Chocolate Crunch Bars

Preparation time: 5 minutes

Cooking time: 5 minutes

Servings: 4

Ingredients:

- 1 1/2 c. sugar-free chocolate chips
- 1 c. almond butter
- Stevia to taste
- 1/4 c. coconut oil
- 3 c. pecans, chopped

Directions:

1. Layer an 8-in. baking pan with parchment paper.

2. Mix the chocolate chips with butter, coconut oil, and sweetener in a bowl.

3. Melt it by heating it in a microwave for 2–3 minutes until well mixed.

4. Stir in nuts and seeds. Mix gently.

5. Pour this batter carefully into the baking pan and spread evenly.

6. Refrigerate for 2–3 hours.

7. Slice and serve.

Per serving: Calories: 316 kcal; Fat: 31 g; Carbs: 8 g; Protein: 6 g; Sugar: 2 g

139. Coconut and Fruit Cake

Preparation time: 10 minutes

Cooking time: 2 hours And 30 minutes

Servings: 2

Ingredients:

- 1 cup mango, peeled and chopped
- 1 and ½ cups whole wheat flour
- ½ cup coconut milk
- 1 cup avocado, peeled, pitted and mashed
- ½ cup coconut flakes, unsweetened
- ½ teaspoon cinnamon powder

Directions:

1. In a regular bowl, mix mango with flour and other ingredients and whisk.

2. Line a slow cooker with parchment paper, pour cake mix and cook on High for 2 hours and 30 minutes.

3. Cool the cake down before slicing and serving it.

Per serving: Calories: 249 kcal; Fat: 12 g; Carbs: 32 g; Protein: 5 g; Sugar: 5 g

140. Berry-Banana Yogurt

Preparation time: 10 minutes

Cooking time: 0 minute

Servings: 1

Ingredients:

- ½ banana, frozen fresh
- 1 container 5.3ounes Greek yogurt, non-fat
- ¼ cup quick-cooking oats
- ½ cup blueberries, fresh and frozen
- 1 cup almond milk
- ¼ cup collard greens, chopped

- 5-6 ice cubes

Directions:

1. Take a microwave-safe cup and add 1 cup almond milk and ¼ cup oats.

2. Place cups in the microwave on high for 2.5 minutes.

3. When oats are cooked, remove them from the oven.

4. Mix them well

5. Add all ingredients to the blender.

6. Blend until a smooth and creamy mixture.

7. Serve chilled and enjoy!

Per serving: Calories: 379 kcal; Fat: 10 g; Carbs: 63 g; Protein: 13 g; Sugar: 1 g

141. Avocado Chocolate Mousse

Preparation time: 10 minutes

Cooking time: 0 minute

Servings: 9

Ingredients:

- 3 ripe avocados,
- 6 ounces of plain Greek yogurt
- 1/8 cup almond milk, unsweetened
- ¼ cup of cocoa powder
- ½ tsp salt
- 2 tbsps. raw honey
- 1 bar dark chocolate
- 1 tsp vanilla extract

Directions:

1. Place all ingredients in the food processor

2. Pulse until smooth

3. Serve chilled and enjoy!

Per serving: Calories: 208 kcal; Fat: 4 g; Carbs: 17 g; Protein: 5 g; Sugar: 10 g

142. Peanut Butter Bars

Preparation time: 10 minutes

Cooking time: 10 minutes

Servings: 6

Ingredients:

- 3/4 c. almond flour

- 2 oz. almond butter
- 1/4 c. Swerve
- 1/2 c. peanut butter
- 1/2 tsp. vanilla

Directions:

1. Combine all the ingredients for the bars.

2. Transfer this mixture to 6-in. small pan. Press it firmly.

3. Refrigerate for 30 minutes.

4. Slice and serve.

Per serving: Calories: 214 kcal; Fat: 19 g; Carbs: 6 g; Protein: 6 g; Sugar: 2 g

143. Coconut Butter Figs

Preparation time: 6 minutes

Cooking time: 2 hours

Servings: 2

Ingredients:

- 1 cup coconut cream
- 12 figs, halved
- 2 tablespoons coconut butter, melted
- ¼ cup palm sugar

Directions:

1. In your slow cooker, mix coconut butter with figs, sugar and cream, stir, cover and cook on High for 2 hours.

2. Divide into bowls and serve cold.

Per serving: Calories: 353 kcal; Fat: 19 g; Carbs: 48 g; Protein: 4 g; Sugar: 36 g

144. Cashews Cake

Preparation time: 10 minutes

Cooking time: 2 hours and 30 minutes

Servings: 2

Ingredients:

- 1 and ½ cups avocado, peeled, pitted and mashed
- ½ cup coconut milk
- ½ cup coconut cream
- ½ teaspoon vanilla extract
- 1 cup cashews, chopped
- 4 tablespoons avocado oil

- Juice of 2 limes
- 2 tablespoons coconut sugar

Directions:

1. In your food processor, Combine avocado with cream and other ingredients and pulse well.

2. Pour this into a slow cooker lined with parchment paper and cook on High for 2 hours and 30 minutes.

3. Slice and serve cold.

Per serving: Calories: 250 kcal; Fat: 19 g; Carbs: 23 g; Protein: 2 g; Sugar: 14 g

145. Dark Chocolate Granola Bars

Preparation time: 10 minutes

Cooking time: 25 minutes

Servings: 12

Ingredients:

- 1 cup tart cherries, dried
- 2 cups buckwheat
- ¼ cup of flaxseed
- 1 cup of walnuts
- 2 eggs
- 1 tsp of salt
- ¼ cup dark cocoa powder
- 2/3 cup honey
- ½ cup dark chocolate chips
- 1 tsp of vanilla

Directions:

1. Preheat oven to 350 degrees F.

2. Apply cooking spray lightly on a baking pan.

3. Pulse together walnuts, wheat, tart cherries, salt, and flaxseed in a food processor. Everything should be chopped fine.

4. Whisk together honey, eggs, vanilla, and cocoa powder in a bowl.

5. Add wheat mix to bowl. Stir to combine well.

6. Include chocolate chips. Stir again.

7. Now pour this mixture into a baking dish.

8. Sprinkle some chocolate chips and tart cherries.

9. Bake for 25 minutes. Set aside cooling bee serving.

Per serving: Calories: 634 kcal; Fat: 28 g; Carbs: 100 g; Protein: 9 g; Sugar: 40 g

146. Kale Flavored Ice Cubes

Preparation time: 4 hours 10 minutes

Cooking time: 0 minutes

Servings: 24

Ingredients:

- Honey (¼ cup)
- Water (Two cups)
- Kale (3 cups, chopped)

Directions:

1. Blend all ingredients.

2. Set a fine-mesh strainer in a bowl. Before transferring your juice into the filter.

3. Gently press the pulp to extract all possible liquid, then discard the pulp.

4. Fill your empty ice trays with your juice.

5. Set to freeze for at least 3 hours until frozen.

6. Keep them in the freezer until ready to serve.

Per serving: Calories: 110 kcal; Fat: 25 g; Carbs: 4 g; Protein: 3 g; Sugar: 3 g

147. Simply Vanilla Frozen Greek Yogurt

Preparation time: 5 minutes + 8 hours to freeze

Cooking time: 0 minutes

Servings: 2-3

Ingredients:

- 4 cups nonfat plain Greek yogurt
- 4 tbsps. vanilla whey Protein powder
- 4 tbsps. vanilla extract
- 4 tsps. stevia or no-calorie sweetener

Directions:

1. In a large bowl or loaf pan, combine yogurt, Protein powder, vanilla extract, and stevia.

2. Cover and freeze overnight or for 8 hours.

3. Serve and enjoy.

Per serving: Calories: 183 kcal; Fat: 1 g; Carbs: 12 g; Protein: 28 g; Sugar: 8 g

148. Raisin Bran Muffins

Preparation time: 15 minutes

Cooking time: 30 minutes

Servings: 36

Ingredients:

- 1 cup boiling water
- 2½ cups All-Bran cereal
- 2½ cups all-purpose flour
- 2½ tsps. baking soda
- 1 tsp salt
- ½ cup vegetable oil
- 1 cup sugar
- 2 eggs, beaten
- 2 cups buttermilk
- 1½ cups raisins
- 1 cup bran flakes

Directions:

1. Set oven to 400°F.

2. Grease a muffin tin. Put boiling water over 1 cup All-Bran, and let sit for 10 minutes.

3. Place baking soda, flour, and salt mix, then set it aside.

4. Stir oil in the bran and water mixture and put the remaining bran, sugar, eggs, and buttermilk.

5. Put flour mixture in bran mixture and mix to combine. Stir raisins and bran flakes, and fill muffin cups ¾ full with batter.

6. Bake muffins for 20 minutes.

Per serving: Calories: 104 kcal; Fat: 4 g; Carbs: 17 g; Protein: 3 g; Sugar: 3 g

149. Maple Syrup and Mint Cream

Preparation time: 10 minutes

Cooking time: 1 Hour

Servings: 2

Ingredients:

- 1 cup almond milk
- 1 tablespoon coconut sugar
- 1 teaspoon maple syrup
- 1 tablespoon mint, chopped
- 1 cup fat-free coconut cream
- 2 teaspoons green tea powder

Directions:

1. In a slow cooker, combine milk with sugar and other ingredients, put the lid on and cook on High for 1 hour.

2. Divide into bowls and serve cold.

Per serving: Calories: 241 kcal; Fat: 16 g; Carbs: 22 g; Protein: 4 g; Sugar: 3 g

150. Yogurt Cheese and Fruit

Preparation time: 10 minutes

Cooking time: 0 minutes

Servings: 6

Ingredients:

- 3 cups plain nonfat yogurt
- 1 tsp fresh lemon juice
- ½ cup orange juice
- ½ cup water
- 1 fresh Golden Delicious apple
- 1 fresh pear
- ¼ cup honey
- ¼ cup dried cranberries or raisins

Directions:

1. Prepare yogurt cheese day bee by lining a colander or strainer with cheesecloth. Scoop yogurt in cheesecloth, place a strainer over a pot or bowl to catch the whey and refrigerate 8 hours before serving.

2. In a huge mixing bowl, mix juices and water. Cut apple, then pear in wedges, place wedges in juice mixture and let it sit for 5 minutes. Strain off liquid.

3. Please remove yogurt from the refrigerator, slice it, and place it on plates when it is firm. Arrange fruit wedges around yogurt. Drizzle with honey and sprinkle with cranberries or raisins before serving.

Per serving: Calories: 177 kcal; Fat: 1 g; Carbs: 35 g; Protein: 6 g; Sugar: 3 g

Conversion Chart

Volume Equivalents (Liquid)

US Standard	US Standard (ounces)	Metric (approximate)
2 tablespoons	1 fl. oz.	30 mL
¼ cup	2 fl. oz.	60 mL
½ cup	4 fl. oz.	120 mL
1 cup	8 fl. oz.	240 mL
1½ cups	12 fl. oz.	355 mL
2 cups or 1 pint	16 fl. oz.	475 mL
4 cups or 1 quart	32 fl. oz.	1 L
1 gallon	128 fl. oz.	4 L

Volume Equivalents (Dry)

US Standard	Metric (approximate)
⅛ teaspoon	0.5 mL
¼ teaspoon	1 mL
½ teaspoon	2 mL
¾ teaspoon	4 mL
1 teaspoon	5 mL
1 tablespoon	15 mL
¼ cup	59 mL
⅓ cup	79 mL
½ cup	118 mL
⅔ cup	156 mL
¾ cup	177 mL
1 cup	235 mL
2 cups or 1 pint	475 mL
3 cups	700 mL
4 cups or 1 quart	1 L

Oven Temperatures

Fahrenheit (F)	Celsius (C) (approximate)
250°F	120°C
300°F	150°C
325°F	165°C
350°F	180°C
375°F	190°C
400°F	200°C

425°F	220°C
450°F	230°C

Weight Equivalents

US Standard	Metric (approximate)
1 tablespoon	15 g
½ ounce	15 g
1 ounce	30 g
2 ounces	60 g
4 ounces	115 g
8 ounces	225 g
12 ounces	340 g
16 ounces or 1 pound	455 g

30-Day Meal Plan

Days	Breakfast	Lunch	Dinner	Dessert
1	Raspberry Almond Oatmeal	Hot & Spicy Shredded Chicken	Spanish Rice	Lemon Vegan Cake
2	German Chocolate Cake Protein Oats	Clean Salmon With Soy Sauce	Lemony Mussels	Avocado Chocolate Mousse
3	Cinnamon Fried Bananas	Black Bean Quesadillas	Chicken With Apples And Potatoes	Dark Chocolate Granola Bars
4	Melting Tuna And Cheese Toasties	Marinated Fish Steaks	Shrimp With Spicy Spinach	Simply Vanilla Frozen Greek Yogurt
5	Chia Chocolate Pudding	Sesame Pork With Mustard Sauce	Sweet Potato and Black Bean Chili	Maple Syrup And Mint Cream
6	Rajun' Cajun Roll-Ups	Mexican Cod Fillets	Italian Bean Soup	Coconut Butter Figs
7	Southwest Deviled Eggs	Spring Soup With Gourmet Grains	Roasted Pork And Apples	Coconut And Fruit Cake
8	Cauliflower Mac & Cheese	Sesame-Tuna Skewers	Shrimp And Corn	Gala Apple Flavored Ice Cubes
9	Simple Steel-Cut Oats	Rosemary Lamb	Spiced Soup With Lentils & Legumes	Shortbread Cookies
10	Whole Grain Pancakes	Scallops With Mushroom Special		Chocolate Cream
11	Sweet Potato Home Fries	Wild Rice With Spicy Chickpeas	Barbecue Beef Brisket	Homemade Protein Bar
12	Flaxseed Banana Muffins	Herbed Harvest Rice	Easy Shrimp	Chocolate Crunch Bars
13	Spicy Avocado Deviled Eggs	Teriyaki Chicken Under Pressure	Maple Rice	Kale Flavored Ice Cubes
14	Perfect Hard-Boiled Eggs	Rosemary-Lemon Cod	Shrimp With Linguine	Raisin Bran Muffins
15	Cranberry Muesli	Coconutty Brown Rice	Chicken Salad Delight	Berry-Banana Yogurt
16	Apple Oats	Pinto Beans	Delicious Creamy Crab Meat	Yogurt Cheese And Fruit
17	Savory Yogurt Bowls	Cajun Chicken And Potatoes	Lemon Chicken And Rice	Cashews Cake
18	Super-Simple Granola	Whitefish Curry	Fried Rice With Kale	Carrot Cake

19	Breakfast Hash	Bean Enchiladas	Creamy Turkey And Mushrooms	Chocolate Chip Quinoa Granola Bars
20	Granola Parfait	Cod With Ginger	Pan-Seared Halibut With Citrus Butter Sauce	Peanut Butter Bars
21	Southwest Deviled Eggs	Mediterranean Lamb Meatballs	Sweetened Brown Rice	Shortbread Cookies
22	Cauliflower Mac & Cheese	Chili Shrimp And Pineapple	Basil Avocado Pasta Salad	Chocolate Cream
23	Simple Steel-Cut Oats	Cauliflower Fried Rice	Slow Cooker Chicken	Homemade Protein Bar
24	Raspberry Almond Oatmeal	Asian Cabbage Salad	Cheesy Garlic Salmon	Dark Chocolate Granola Bars
25	German Chocolate Cake Protein Oats	Coconut-Curry Chicken	Slow Cooker Boston Beans	Simply Vanilla Frozen Greek Yogurt
26	Cinnamon Fried Bananas	Healthy Halibut Fillets	Roasted Root Vegetables	Maple Syrup And Mint Cream
27	Melting Tuna And Cheese Toasties	Wild Rice Harvest Soup	Beef And Asparagus	Coconut Butter Figs
28	Cranberry Muesli	Cauliflower Rice	Simple Salmon With Eggs	Shortbread Cookies
29	Apple Oats	Italian Beef	Green Beans Greek Style	Chocolate Cream
30	Savory Yogurt Bowls	Salmon And Roasted Peppers	Pureed Classic Egg Salad	Lemon Vegan Cake

Index

Melting Tuna and Cheese Toasties; 23
Mexican Cod Fillets; 46
Moch Mashed Potatoes; 62
No Dish Summer Medley; 59
Nutty and Fruity Garden Salad; 38
Pan-Seared Halibut with Citrus Butter Sauce; 48
Peanut Butter Bars; 67
Perfect Hard-boiled Eggs; 18
Pickle Roll-Ups; 58
Pinto Beans; 25
Potato nd Broccoli Soup; 55
Pureed Classic Egg Salad; 37
Quick Miso Soup with Wilted Greens; 52
Raisin Bran Muffins; 69
Rajun' Cajun Roll-Ups; 19
Raspberry Almond Oatmeal; 18
Red Soup, Seville Style; 56
Roasted Beet Salad; 34
Roasted Garden Vegetables; 34
Roasted Pork and Apples; 43
Roasted Root Vegetables; 35
Roasted Vegetable Soup; 54
Root Vegetable Soup; 53
Rosemary Lamb; 40
Rosemary-Lemon Cod; 50
Salad Bites; 33
Salmon and Roasted Peppers; 47
Savory Yogurt Bowls; 21
Scallops with Mushroom Special; 48
Sesame Pork with Mustard Sauce; 41
Sesame-Tuna Skewers; 47
Shortbread Cookies; 64

Shrimp and Corn; 47
Shrimp with Linguine; 51
Shrimp with Spicy Spinach; 45
Simple Salmon with Eggs; 45
Simple Steel-Cut Oats; 23
Simply Vanilla Frozen Greek Yogurt; 68
Slow Cooker Boston Beans; 25
Slow Cooker Chicken; 41
Southwest Deviled Eggs; 20
Spanish Rice; 29
Spiced Soup with Lentils & Legumes; 30
Spicy Avocado Deviled Eggs; 18
Spicy Carrot Soup; 56
Spinach and Artichoke Dip; 59
Spring Soup with Gourmet Grains; 27
Steamed Asparagus; 61
Super Green Soup; 53
Super-Simple Granola; 22
Sweet Potato Home Fries; 21
Sweet Potato nd Black Bean Chili; 25
Sweetened Brown Rice; 26
Tenderloin Grilled Salad; 32
Teriyaki Chicken Under Pressure; 42
Thai Quinoa Salad; 35
Tomato nd Cabbage Puree Soup; 54
Tomato nd Mozzarella Bites; 58
Tomato, Basil, and Cucumber Salad; 32
Whitefish Curry; 49
Whole Grain Pancakes; 23
Wild Rice Harvest Soup; 26
Wild Rice with Spicy Chickpeas; 28
Yogurt Cheese and Fruit; 69

Conclusion

The number of people with diabetes continues to rise across the globe due to the hectic modern lifestyle, what we eat, stressful workplaces and the aging population. The rapid rise of diabetic cases has fortunately been curtailed recently due to better co-ordinations amongst the national health organizations.

It is becoming paramount to handle diabetes and create platforms where people with diabetes can come for practical solutions and have a more fulfilling life. This book has shown you some practical programs to prevent and reverse diabetes.

The occurrence of type 2 diabetes has been better controlled in recent years due to preventive measures taken from widespread education. Hospitals and other healthcare authorities are spreading the word about diabetes in schools, offices and public places. The selection of foods and drinks for students in schools or higher educational institutions has been improved to ensure students grow up with better habits in food consumption.

Tackling diabetes in advanced countries has been through practical measures that people suffering from the disease can go on their own such as daily exercises, healthy eating, imbibing healthy habits and taking the correct dosage of medication consistently on time.

Made in the USA
Columbia, SC
23 March 2023

14161923R00043